COMMON SENSE ABOUT

SMOKING

C. M. *Fletcher*

Harvey Cole

Lena Jeger

Christopher Wood

PENGUIN BOOKS
BALTIMORE · MARYLAND

Penguin Books Ltd, Harmondsworth, Middlesex
U.S.A.: Penguin Books Inc., 3300 Clipper Mill Road, Baltimore 11, Md
AUSTRALIA: Penguin Books Pty Ltd, 762 Whitehorse Road,
Mitcham, Victoria

First published 1963

Copyright © Penguin Books and contributors, 1963

Made and printed in Great Britain
by Hunt, Barnard & Co. Ltd, Aylesbury
Set in Intertype Plantin

CONTENTS

1234297

THE MEDICAL EVIDENCE

C. M. Fletcher

It does not require a scientist to prove that smoking has a powerful attraction for many people. The remarkable thing is the way this attraction can overcome the natural aversion that most animals, including humans, have for inhaling smoke. The smoke of the first tobaccos imported into this country was much ranker than the elegant aromatic smoke of the modern cigarette, and yet within a few years of its importation its use had spread so widely that it was taxed by Queen Elizabeth. Ever since tobacco was introduced into the Western world more and more people have come to use it and now three quarters of the men and half the women in this country are smokers.

The immediate effects of smoking in the uninitiated are dramatic – a racing pulse, nausea, and often vomiting, yet despite this unpleasant experience the majority of those who have once experimented notice some indefinable pleasure whose attraction is so strong that they persist in their attempts. They soon overcome the immediate unpleasant effects by habituation and become so devoted to the habit that if they are separated from it they become distracted and miserable. Indeed the misery of the smoker divorced from his tobacco, the intensity of his relief when he is re-united, and the remarkable black market in cigarettes that pervaded Europe in the post-war years justify the use of the word addiction to describe the relationship of most smokers to their tobacco.

It is not surprising that such addiction has been a perpetual source of controversy. While its devotees have praised it as indispensable for social intercourse, for work, and for relaxation, its critics have decried the litter, malodour, expense, and abandon associated with the habit. Even smokers admit to some minor ill-effects: 'that it is bad for the wind' and that it makes them cough, and they fear its effects sufficiently to forbid its pleasure to their children, often on the unsupported idea that it might arrest their growth.

For centuries doctors have taken part in this debate according to their own habits. Those who are smokers have condoned and those who are non-smokers have condemned the habit, but without any sound evidence in support of either side. Its supporters, of course, needed no scientific evidence. If a man says he enjoys a habit, that it helps him to work and soothes the paths of social intercourse he needs no proof to support his claim. It is the detractors who must seek evidence in support of their opposition, but until recently there was little evidence that smoking had any serious consequences. Cancer of the lip was thought to be associated with smoking of clay pipes but these went out of fashion and the tremendous growth of tobacco consumption, in particular of cigarettes, which took place throughout the first half of this century proceeded with no protest of any weight from doctors.

Yet today the position is entirely different. Smoking, in particular of cigarettes, is now regarded by doctors as an important cause of a wide variety of serious diseases. There are two main reasons for this recent revolution in medical opinion. First, there has been a steady change from smoking of pipes and cigars to smoking of cigarettes during this century and particularly since the First World War. It is cigarettes that appear to be dangerous, but since their ill-effects take some twenty or thirty years to declare themselves they have only recently become widely manifest.

Secondly, it is only fairly recently that medical research has developed adequate techniques by which the medical effects of environment and habits can be measured.

Doctors have increasingly begun to understand and use these statistical scientific methods, and to rely upon such evidence rather than upon the personal experiences and prejudices of individual physicians to judge the effects of smoking. In the past fifty years medicine has become much more a science while still remaining an art and a craft.

It is notable that this change in medical opinion about smoking has hitherto had little effect on smoking habits. A series of firm pronouncements by the Medical Research Council, by the Ministry of Health, and recently by the Royal College of Physicians have been made calling attention to the evidence that cigarette smoking may be dangerous, and yet on each occasion there has been no more than a momentary fall in tobacco sales before the steady rise in cigarette consumption that has characterized the past decades has been resumed. In contrast to this, there has been a great change in the smoking habits of doctors. There used to be little difference between the habits of doctors and the general public, but the last ten years have changed this. Two-thirds of the general public smoke cigarettes but only just over one-third of doctors. More than half of all doctors are non-smokers but only a quarter of the general public. Among doctors who specialize in chest diseases cigarette smoking has become extremely uncommon. At a recent meeting of 200 such doctors lasting for two and a half hours in a lecture theatre equipped with ashtrays, only three cigarettes were seen to be smoked.

It is not, perhaps, surprising that pronouncements by the Government should have had no more effect upon the general public than have the prohibitions of school masters upon their pupils. Doctors have often been wrong in the past. The tobacco manufacturers have disputed the evidence in public and have quoted eminent scientists in their support. The evidence appears in any case to be 'mere statistics' and surely anyone can prove anything by figures: so the smokers argue. What is to be done? The first thing is to look carefully at the evidence, shorn of its technicalities, and try to see how convincing it is. In doing this we shall have to think about the real meaning of 'a cause of a disease'. This is an idea which is not quite as simple as it might seem at first. When the evidence has been reviewed we must decide whether anything should be done to prevent any harm that smoking may do.

But first what is the evidence?

SMOKING AND LUNG CANCER

We must start with lung cancer because it was the remarkable increase in the death-rate from lung cancer in countries all over the world which really started the intensive research into the effects of cigarette smoking that has taken place during the last ten years. Forty years ago lung cancer was a rare disease. In England and Wales in 1920 only 309 deaths in men and 191 deaths in women were attributed to this disease. By 1930 there were 2,258 deaths in men and 864 in women, and in 1960 the enormous total was 18,882 in men and 3,118 in women.

A curious feature of the increasing death-rates is shown in Figure 1. Here death-rates from lung cancer at various ages from thirty to eighty are plotted for men born in successive quinquennia from 1856–61 onwards. It will be seen that the older men have had relatively low death-rates even up to an advanced age. It is the men born in more recent years who have suffered a steadily increasing death-rate at all ages. The two most recent generations are beginning to look much alike. This striking increase in death-rates and the different rates for the different generations cannot be due to some change in human heredity making each generation more liable to lung cancer than its predecessor. Hereditary changes do not occur as rapidly as this. It must be due to some new factor in the environment to which each generation has become increasingly exposed. One possibility that has been suggested is that doctors have become increasingly inclined to diagnose lung cancer in cases which they would previously have diagnosed as being due to some other condition, some other form of cancer for instance, or perhaps even tuberculosis. No experienced pathologist or chest physician will readily accept this explanation. Lung cancer can very rarely be confused with tuberculosis. Some cases of lung cancer twenty or thirty years ago were certainly mistakenly diagnosed as cancer of the liver or stomach and a switch of diagnoses in this way may account for the fact that death-rates from these forms of cancer have been declining as lung cancer has increased. But there is one fact which is quite impossible to explain this way and that is that the death-rate for lung cancer has been increasing much faster in men than in women. Exactly the same standards of diagnosis are applied to both sexes, so that there must have been some real change, a real and very great increase, in the number of people affected by this disease.

It must be concluded that during this century each generation has been exposed to some new influence, affecting the lungs, to which previous generations have not been exposed. Cigarette smoking is just such an agent and a vast amount of investigation has led to the conclusion that it is probably the chief cause of lung cancer.

Retrospective studies

The first and simplest sort of investigation carried out was to take hospital patients suffering from lung cancer and

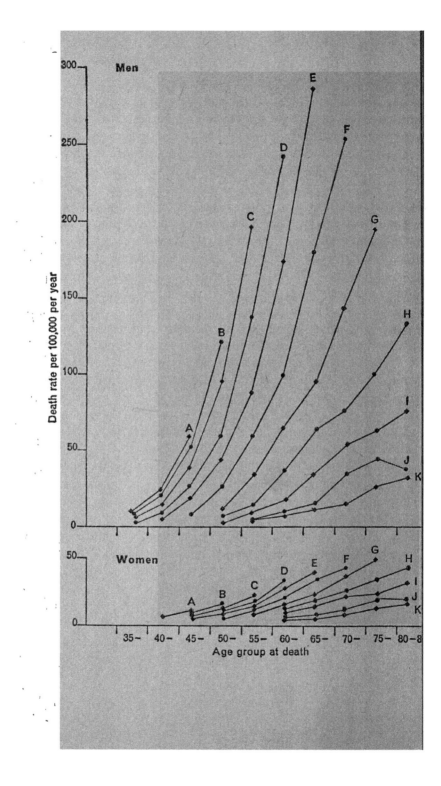

for each patient to choose another patient suffering from some other disease of the same age and sex, and to record the smoking habits of these patients. More than thirty studies of this kind have been done in at least ten different countries, and all of them have shown that there are more heavy cigarette smokers and fewer light cigarette smokers and non-smokers among the lung-cancer cases than among the others. All the investigations of this kind have agreed with this finding. A number of criticisms have been made of this sort of study: for instance, that investigators may in some way have exaggerated the smoking habits of those they knew to have lung cancer; or that the cancer patients themselves may have given an inaccurate account of their past smoking habits; or that the control cases may in some way have had smoking habits that were not really representative of the general population. All these criticisms can be

Figure 1. Death-rates from lung cancer according to age in men and women born at various periods:

A=born around 1906	G=born around 1876
B= „ „ 1901	H= „ „ 1871
C= „ „ 1896	I= „ „ 1866
D= „ „ 1891	J= „ „ 1861
E= „ „ 1886	K= „ „ 1856
F= „ „ 1881	

Each 'cohort' of men born in successive five-year periods since 1856 has shown a greater mortality from lung cancer at each five-year period of life than the previous 'cohort'. The difference between the most recent cohorts A and B seems to be getting less than that between the earlier cohorts.

The same analysis of death-rates for women shows a much lower mortality rate. The same sort of change has been occurring in the past fifty years, but to a much smaller degree.

No other form of cancer has shown an increasing death-rate from cohort to cohort like lung cancer.

(The figure is taken from *Carcinoma of the Lung*, ed. J. R. Bignall, Livingstone, 1958.)

answered and it is difficult to see how any systematic bias of any kind could have produced such uniform results in so many independent investigations.

Prospective studies

Convincing confirmatory evidence has been obtained by surveys of a more reliable type. In these the smoking habits of large numbers of men have been recorded; the men have subsequently been observed over several years and the causes of all the deaths occurring among them have been recorded. Three such investigations of this kind have been fully reported. One carried out by Sir Austin Bradford Hill and Dr Richard Doll among British doctors, and two in America, among friends of volunteer workers of the American Cancer Society and among Government life-insurance policy holders. These studies have all shown that cigarette smokers have a much higher death-rate than smokers of pipes or cigars and that non-smokers have the lowest death-rate. We shall return to consider the general increase in death-rates later on, but in particular these studies have all shown a steep increase in numbers of deaths from lung cancer with increasing cigarette consumption. This striking relationship between lung-cancer deaths and numbers of cigarettes smoked has been similar in all the three studies and it is illustrated in Figure 2. The death-rate from lung cancer in the heavier smokers is twenty to thirty times greater than among non-smokers. It is to be noted that the death-rate from lung cancer in Great Britain is the highest in the world and Figure 2 shows that the mortality rate at each level of cigarette consumption is greater in the British than in the American studies. Two possible explanations for this have been advanced; one that the British are exposed to higher levels of general air pollu-

ion, and secondly that they tend to smoke their cigarettes
o a shorter butt-length so that for each cigarette consumed
hey are exposed to greater quantities of smoke.

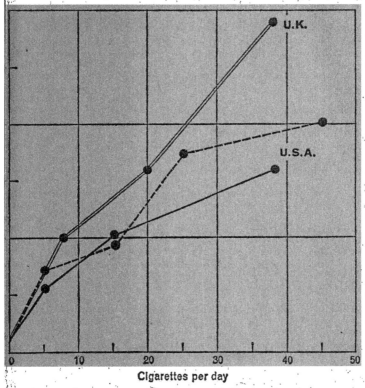

Cigarettes per day

Figure 2. The relationship between the numbers of cigarettes
moked per day and lung-cancer death-rates in three prospective
tudies. The figure shows how much the risk of getting lung cancer
vas found to be multiplied in those who smoked various numbers of
igarettes per day at the beginning of the survey in comparison with
he risk of non-smokers. The first horizontal line in the figure in-
licates ten times the risk of non-smokers, the second one twenty
imes, and the third one thirty times. The figures are derived from
)oll and Hill's study of British doctors in Great Britain and from
he studies of American men by Hammond and Horn and by Dorn.

These studies also established two other important facts. First, the death-rate in pipe smokers is much lower than that in cigarette smokers though rather higher than in non-smokers. In the American studies, where there were enough pure cigar smokers for analysis, it was found that they had the same incidence of lung cancer as the non-smokers. Secondly, those who had given up smoking some time before the beginning of the study had lung-cancer death-rates lower than those who had continued to smoke the same amounts. Those who had given up for more than ten years had about a quarter and those who had given up for less than ten years about a half of the lung-cancer mortality of continuing smokers. Giving up smoking seems to lessen the risk.

It has been objected to these studies, as to the earlier ones, that there may have been some bias introduced by the selection of subjects for the study. Those who were willing to respond to the questionnaire about smoking habits could have been different in some way from those who did not respond, so that, for instance, the healthier non-smokers, proud of their abstinence, may have been more willing to respond than those who were iller, while the healthier smokers did not respond because they were indifferent. Thus the iller non-smokers and healthier smokers might have been excluded. The initial state of health of the subjects could only effect mortality rates during the first one or two years of the study, however, and in all the studies the association between lung cancer and smoking became closer as time went by. Error might also have been caused if, with increasing interest in the association between cigarette smoking and lung cancer, doctors had been more ready to diagnose lung cancer in people who smoked cigarettes, and tended to avoid the diagnosis in non-smokers. This tendency would have been inclined to increase the mortality

rate from other causes among non-smokers and to decrease
it in the smokers, and yet, in all the studies, it was found
that the death-rate from all causes was greater in smokers
than non-smokers. Moreover when the association was
looked at only in those cases of lung cancer which had been
positively verified by post-mortem examination, the link
with smoking was even closer than in the cases as a whole,
so that diagnostic error tended to reduce the association with
smoking in the whole study.

No one now denies that these studies have proved that
there is a close association between cigarette smoking and
lung cancer. This must be accepted, but we have to consider whether this association is due to cigarette smoking
causing lung cancer, or whether there is some other
explanation.

The theory that cigarette smoking causes lung cancer
would imply that there are substances in the smoke capable
of causing cancer. In fact, analysis of cigarette smoke has
shown that there are a considerable number of compounds
in it which are known to be capable of causing cancer
when they are applied to the skin of animals in laboratory
experiments. These substances are, however, present in such
small amounts in cigarette smoke that they would not be
likely to have much effect in the concentrations in which
they occur in smoke without some other influence. Laboratory experiments have shown that the ability of these substances to cause cancer can be greatly increased by other
irritating substances known as 'co-carcinogens' and that
there are a number of substances in cigarette smoke which
can act in this way, so that the combined effect of these
substances in the smoke could well be cancer-producing.

It is true that no one has yet produced lung cancer in
laboratory animals by exposing them to the inhalation of
cigarette smoke, but it appears to require at least twenty

years' exposure to cigarette smoke in the human being before lung cancer is likely to develop and no experimental animal can be exposed for this length of time. The laboratory evidence is thus equivocal.

A chronic irritating effect of tobacco smoke should produce changes in the bronchial tubes of smokers and we should expect to find more severe changes in the heavier smokers. This has been found to be the case in a number of investigations in which the bronchial tubes of people who had died from all sorts of diseases have been examined and the findings have been related to their smoking habits during life. In the heavier smokers chronic changes of inflammation and degeneration can be found more often and in greater severity than in lighter smokers and non-smokers and some pathologists consider that these changes are of a kind that may be precursors of cancer, although this is not universally agreed.

If cigarette smoke is a cause of cancer, those who inhale the smoke should have a higher incidence of the disease than those who do not inhale. This question has so far only been investigated in four retrospective inquiries. In three of them there were more inhalers among the lung-cancer patients than the controls, but the British study by Doll and Hill was an exception especially in heavier smokers. Here there were more inhalers among the control patients than among the lung-cancer patients. It is difficult to be certain what this one exception means, but it may be due simply to the fact that smokers do not always know whether they do or do not inhale and to the fact that almost all heavy smokers do inhale to some extent.

These independent pieces of evidence give additional support to the causative theory, but before we accept it we must consider any other possible explanations which will fit both the association between lung cancer and smoking and the increase in mortality in recent years. A number of other theories have been put forward:

1. It has been suggested that early in life some change may take place in the bronchial tube which may develop into cancer thirty or forty years later and which produces a desire to smoke. No such process is known to medical science and this theory would demand that this change had for some unknown reason only become prevalent during recent years and that it caused a desire for cigarettes rather than pipes. No one can seriously maintain this theory.

2. It has been suggested that cigarette smokers who die of lung cancer would in any case have died of some other form of cancer and that smoking may only switch a liability of cancer from other organs to the lungs. If this were so, cigarette smokers should show a decreased mortality from other forms of cancer. This has not been observed in any of the prospective surveys, indeed cigarette smokers have a slightly higher mortality from cancer outside the lungs than do non-smokers.

3. It has been suggested that those cigarette smokers who die from lung cancer are born with 'weak lungs' so that they in former days would have died from tuberculosis, which used to be much more prevalent. Since the death-rate from tuberculosis has declined in recent years, the theory postulates, these people with weak lungs survive only to die of lung cancer. This theory does not explain the association between cigarette smoking and lung cancer and there is no evidence that susceptibility to tuberculosis and to lung cancer are related. Further, although tuberculous mortality has fallen faster in women than in men, lung cancer has increased more rapidly in men than in women.

4. The most serious alternative theory that has been advanced is supported among others by the late Sir Ronald Fisher, the eminent statistician. He suggested that the desire to smoke is inherited and that those who inherit this desire

also inherit a liability to lung cancer. It is known that smoking habits are to some extent determined by heredity, for it has been found that the smoking habits of identical twins, who have exactly the same inherited constitution, are more similar than are the smoking habits of non-identical twins or ordinary brothers. Although there is no hereditary liability to most forms of cancer there are some forms which do run in families and it is possible that susceptibility to lung cancer may be inherited. This theory would account for the fact that people who give up smoking have a lower cancer mortality than those who continue to smoke because those able to give up smoking would presumably be hereditarily intermediate between smokers and non-smokers. To explain the tremendous increase in lung cancer that has occurred in the last fifty years, it is necessary to add to this theory the supposition that there is some other unidentified cancer-producing influence which has increased simultaneously in twenty or more countries all over the world in which lung-cancer mortality has been increasing. The supporters of this theory have not been able to suggest what this world-wide influence could possibly be. Fisher suggested it might be air pollution, but in most countries pollution has been declining and lung-cancer mortality has increased alike in town and country and in the less as well as in the more polluted countries. The theory is thus inherently unsatisfactory and there is one ingenious investigation which has practically dismissed it. In California there are large numbers of Seventh Day Adventists all of whom are non-smokers, and the incidence of cancer among them has been compared with the other residents of California. Among the male Adventists lung-cancer mortality was one-eighth of that found in the general population of California. There were in fact only two male Adventists who had died of lung cancer and these were both converts who had been

cigarette smokers until middle age. The hereditary explanation of the association between smoking and lung cancer
would thus demand that there is simultaneous inheritance
of the desire to smoke cigarettes, of a liability to lung
cancer, and of a liability not to be born into but to be converted to Seventh Day Adventism. This is quite absurd.

The only way in which the association between lung
cancer and smoking and the increasing mortality from the
disease can be adequately explained is by supposing that
cigarette smoking is a cause of lung cancer. But before we
accept this conclusion we must look carefully to see if there
are any important conflicting facts.

We have already mentioned the fact that one investigation, but only one, failed to observe an increased incidence
of lung cancer in those who said they inhaled smoke compared with those who denied inhaling, but since three other
investigations have shown the expected relationship with
inhaling this objection is invalid.

Figure 3 shows that although there is the close relationship between cigarette consumption in 1930 and death-rates
twenty years later from lung cancer, in countries for which
both sets of figures are available (which the causation
theory would demand), the death-rates for Japan and for
the U.S.A. are lower in relation to the cigarette consumption than in other countries. One explanation of the relatively low death-rate in the U.S.A. may be the fact, already
mentioned, that Americans tend to throw away their
cigarettes before they have smoked them right to the end.
The low rate in Japan remains unexplained but no detailed
study has yet been made of Japanese smoking habits.

We have already mentioned the fact that death-rates from
lung cancer have been rising less steeply in women than in
men during the past forty years and yet it is obvious that
women have increased their cigarette consumption in recent

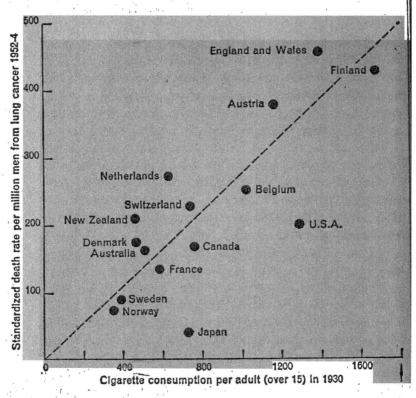

Figure 3. The relationship between lung-cancer mortality in the years 1952–4 and cigarette consumption twenty years previously in fifteen different countries.

years much more rapidly than men. Unfortunately we have no really accurate figures for the amount of cigarettes smoked by women or by men many years ago, but the available figures suggest that men began smoking cigarettes round about 1890 and have steadily increased their consumption since then with high peaks during the war periods. Women on the other hand hardly smoked cigarettes at all until 1920 and few women smoked until shortly before the last war. Even now women, especially the elderly who are most susceptible to cancer, are much lighter smokers than men. One would not expect death-rates from lung cancer to have effected women as severely as men as yet. In fact, the ratio of male to female lung-cancer death-rates is beginning to decrease in the young age-groups as would be expected if the relatively recent adoption of cigarette smoking by younger women was beginning to take effect.

Lastly there is the curious fact that cancer of the windpipe is rare, and cancer starting in the larger bronchial tube is if anything less common than cancer starting in the more peripheral parts of the lung. One would expect the windpipe and the larger bronchial tubes to receive a much higher concentration of smoke than the peripheral parts. There is no explanation for this anomaly but it is known that similar tissues in different parts of the body may respond quite differently to the same agents of disease.

Conclusions

We must conclude that the strong association between cigarette smoking and lung cancer is most readily and most plausibly explained by supposing that it is due to cause and effect so that cigarette smoking is a cause of lung cancer. It is important to remember just what is meant by 'a cause of a disease'. We do not actually know the exact cause of any form of cancer and exactly how or why cells change their normal state of regular growth, begin multiplying riotously, and spread throughout the body destroying and invading other tissues. All we can conclude from the evidence about cigarette smoking is that for some reason or other smoking cigarettes increases the liability of the cells in the bronchial tubes to undergo this malignant change. Nor does our conclusion mean that all smokers get lung cancer: indeed only a minority get it. The study of Doll and Hill of British doctors showed that the total risk of dying of lung cancer for a man who smokes twenty-five or more cigarettes a day

is only one in fourteen before the age of seventy-five, and
one in nine before the age of eighty-five. The risk of those
who smoke smaller numbers of cigarettes is proportionately
less. Nor does our conclusion mean that cigarette smoking
is the only cause of lung cancer. There is quite clear evidence
that exposure to air pollution in our towns and cities increases the risk of smoking cigarettes. There are cancer-
producing substances in coal smoke and it appears that
smoke in cities may combine with cigarette smoke to increase the liability to lung cancer. However, even in our
smoky cities the death-rate from lung cancer among non-
smokers is small, namely about one per 2,000 men aged
thirty-five to seventy-four per annum which is about two
and a half times the rate in rural areas. On the other hand,
the death-rate among heavy cigarette smokers is some thirty
or forty times greater than in non-smokers.

What further proof of the relationship between cigarette
smoking and the disease is required? Ultimate and irrefut-
able proof that cigarettes caused lung cancer could only be
obtained by the wholly impossible experiment of forcing
some 10,000 young children to smoke and to continue to
smoke throughout their lives while forcibly preventing
another 10,000 from smoking cigarettes and to contrast the
causes of death in the two groups. No further experiments
on animals could provide any proof more cogent than the
experiment, however imperfect it may have been, that our
present generation has carried out on itself by its widespread
adoption of cigarette smoking. No animal experiment, indeed, can ever irrefutably demonstrate the cause of any
human disease. Further experimental work among animals
might, however, throw more light on the particular substances in cigarette smoke that may be responsible for its
cancer-producing effect and this might permit the development of forms of tobacco that might be safer. But the safety

of such cigarettes could not be shown until a whole generation of humans had smoked them and no other form of
cigarettes, while others continued to smoke the old-fashioned
sort, and the death-rates from lung cancer had been shown
to be similar in these two groups.

Meanwhile we do know that pipe and cigar smoking produces a very small risk of lung cancer; we do not know why
this is, for the smoke of pipes and cigars contains as many
cancer-producing substances as does the smoke of cigarettes.
The probable explanation is that pipe and cigar smokers
seldom inhale the smoke. This in turn is probably because
the smoke of cigars and most pipes is alkaline, which makes
it more irritating than the slightly acid smoke of cigarettes.

That cigarettes cause lung cancer implies that if the habit
of smoking cigarettes were to cease the death-rate from lung
cancer would eventually fall to a fraction: perhaps, among
men, to only one-tenth of the present level. Since the present annual number of deaths attributed to lung cancer
among men is some 25,000, half of which occur before the
age of retirement, the question is one of enormous personal
and national importance.

SMOKING AND OTHER DISEASES OF THE LUNGS

Chronic bronchitis

The general impression that most smokers have a cough
has been fully confirmed in many population studies.
These have shown that pipe smokers cough much less. Indeed, an early-morning cough, often with the production of
phlegm, is so usual among smokers that it is not regarded as
abnormal. But people with perfectly healthy bronchial tubes
do not cough. The smoker's cough is due to chronic irritation. His phlegm is due to continual over-activity of the
glands in the bronchial tubes which normally produce a fine

film of mucus on the surface of the tubes to trap dust and germs that are inhaled. This film is constantly swept upwards towards the throat by the beating of minute hair-like projections from the cells lining the surface of the tubes, and thus foreign material is removed. If too much mucus is produced the efficiency of this protective mechanism is impaired In most smokers the irritative cough and production of phlegm is harmless, if annoying. But in some the excessive phlegm appears to reduce the efficiency of the bronchial tubes' defences against infection so that recurrent attacks of bronchitis occur in which the phlegm becomes yellow because there is pus in it. This chronic irritation may also lead, in a way we do not fully understand, to a narrowing of the tubes so that the patient – for this is what he has now become – finds it increasingly difficult to breathe. At the same time the actual substance of the lung, the minute air cells in which the blood takes up oxygen from the air, lose their elasticity and break down, and this makes the breathlessness still worse. This is the condition of chronic bronchitis and emphysema which is one of the most common seriously disabling and killing diseases in Great Britain. The death-rate from this disease is higher in this country than in any other country in the world. Nearly ten per cent of all deaths in middle-aged men here are due to it – nearly 6,000 deaths each year in men of working age, but only a quarter of this figure in women.

This distressing disease almost never occurs in non-smokers, which leaves little doubt that smoking, especially of cigarettes, is at least a major predisposing cause of it. But there are other causes. The disease is much commoner in towns than in the country and in the poorer than in the richer sections of society (the bronchitis death-rate in un-skilled labourers is five times as great as in the professional classes), and there are some occupations which seem to increase its incidence. None of these differences can be accounted for by differences in smoking habits. But in town and country and in all occupations, the men and women, both rich and poor, with severe bronchitis have been or are cigarette smokers. The difference in the incidence of the disease between men and women can be largely explained by the difference in cigarette consumption between the sexes.

General air pollution is probably one of the most important causes of bronchitis, and there must be other factors which we do not yet understand which account for the social class differences and for the exceptionally wide prevalence of the disease in this country. When these factors have been identified their control might be more effective in preventing bronchitis than avoidance of cigarettes could ever be. But at present the only way in which the individual can ensure he does not acquire the disease is not to smoke cigarettes.

A simple smoker's cough usually stops completely if no more cigarettes are smoked, but more advanced changes in the bronchial tubes and damage to the lung that causes breathlessness are usually irreversible. Although further damage may be avoided by giving up cigarette smoking, preventive action must be taken early in the disease if it is to be effective.

Pulmonary tuberculosis

This disease, which used to be one of the most serious affections of the lungs in this country, is now readily treated by modern antibiotics and its incidence and its power to kill have been dropping steeply in recent years. Within a generation it should become extremely rare. How far its incidence is affected by smoking is uncertain, for the question has not been widely studied. When patients admitted to hospital because of tuberculosis have been compared with those admitted for other diseases, it has been found that the tuberculous are the heavier smokers, but they are usually heavier drinkers too, and in one study the association of tuberculosis with consumption of alcohol was much closer than with that of tobacco. It may be that the sort of people who smoke and drink heavily are the sort of people who are more susceptible to tuberculosis. The question is unresolved. But most doctors feel that it is bad for anyone with a chronic lung disease to persist in a habit which makes them cough.

No other important lung diseases appear to be associated with smoking, although pneumonia is more prevalent and more likely to be serious in patients with chronic bronchitis. Asthma is no more common in smokers than non-smokers.

SMOKING AND HEART DISEASE

Diseases of the heart, and in particular coronary heart disease, are the most frequent causes of death in middle-aged and elderly people in all Western countries. Coronary heart disease means that the coronary arteries that supply the heart itself with blood are obstructed by encrustation of their walls with fatty deposits called atheroma, or by blood clot. A blood clot is known as a thrombus, and clotting in a coronary artery is known as coronary thrombosis. If a major coronary artery is acutely obstructed the heart is said to be 'infarcted' and the condition is described as a 'cardiac infarct' or 'coronary infarct'. Sudden death may result if a large part of the heart has its circulation obstructed. In patients who survive the acute attack there is usually severe pain in the chest lasting for many hours. In some cases when the blood supply to the heart is sufficient at rest but inadequate for exercise, pain in the chest only comes on on exertion. When the blood supply becomes inadeqate even at rest heart failure may occur. Before the menopause women are affected by this disease much less often than men: thereafter the incidence is similar in both sexes.

During the past thirty or forty years coronary heart disease appears to have been on the increase, especially among middle-aged men in Western countries. Many factors associated with increasing affluence have been advanced to explain this increase: for example, overeating and mental stress. One such factor is the increase in cigarette smoking and this has been widely studied.

It is well known that in some patients with coronary heart disease smoking may bring on pain like that experienced on exertion. This is not surprising for it has been clearly shown in the laboratory that smoking, presumably owing to the effect of nicotine, makes the heart beat faster and increases the work it has to do. But this aggravation of a symptom does not mean that smoking is a cause of the underlying abnormality in the coronary arteries. In all the prospective studies of causes of deaths in relation to smoking habits, however, an association between deaths from coronary heart disease and cigarette smoking has been noted. This is more marked in younger than older men. Those who have given up smoking before the study started have had death-rates intermediate between the cigarette smokers and the non-smokers.

But the situation here is quite different from that of lung cancer. Lung cancer is very rare in non-smokers and thirty to forty times as frequent in the heaviest cigarette smokers. Coronary heart disease is common in non-smokers and only two and a half times more frequent in the heavier smokers. Cigarette smoking cannot therefore be a major cause of coronary heart disease: it could at most be in some way an aggravating factor, and it may not even be this. The association may be simply due to an association between smoking

and other factors that affect the disease – such as mental
strain, sedentary occupation, and even eating fatty foods (of
which smokers have been shown to consume more than non-
smokers). The fact that two studies have shown an association between coronary heart disease and inhalation certainly
suggests a direct effect of smoking, but even this is no proof
– those who inhale may be different sorts of people from
those who do not.

It is very difficult to see how smoking could increase
liability to the degeneration of the arteries which is the basis
of coronary heart disease. It is, however, conceivable that it
could increase the fatality of attacks of coronary thrombosis.
Death in these attacks is often due to an irregular rhythm
of the heart and nicotine has been shown to increase the
tendency of the heart to beat irregularly. It is possible that
a coronary infarct in a smoker with nicotine in his system
might more often have a fatal outcome than in a nicotine-
free non-smoker.

We must conclude that the case against smoking in relation to heart disease is unproven, but a strong suspicion
remains that cigarette smoking does increase the risk from
this disease.

Smoking and other diseases of the circulation

Smoking does not cause high blood pressure; indeed, on
the average, the blood pressure of smokers tends to be
rather lower than that of non-smokers. There is, however,
one fairly uncommon disease of the arteries (thrombo-
angiitis obliterans) in which the flow of blood is impaired,
particularly in the legs. This occurs almost exclusively
among smokers and the symptoms and progression of the
disease are definitely made worse by smoking. This is
presumably because of the effect of nicotine which does
reduce blood flow in the limbs even of normal people.

SMOKING AND VARIOUS OTHER DISEASES

Some *other forms of cancer* than lung cancer have been found to affect smokers more often than non-smokers. Cancers of the mouth, throat, and gullet are among these and affect cigarette, pipe, and cigar smokers more often than non-smokers. But these forms of cancer are also related to alcoholic excess, which is commoner in smokers than non-smokers, so that it is difficult to be sure which is responsible. Curiously, cancer of the bladder in men is also commoner in smokers than non-smokers and in one study there was a definite association between this cancer and inhalation of cigarette smoke. It is difficult to interpret this finding. If it is cause and effect some cancer-reducing substance must be absorbed from the lung and excreted in the urine, but no such substance has yet been identified.

While 4,561 men and 2,606 women died of cancer of the mouth, throat, gullet, and bladder in 1960, only a very small proportion of these deaths could be attributed to smoking.

The symptoms of *gastric and duodenal ulcer* are often made worse by smoking, which in some people increases the acid secreted in the stomach. There is no doubt that the rate of healing of gastric ulcers is slower in patients who continue to smoke than in those who stop, and the death-rate from stomach ulcers is higher in smokers of all kinds than in non-smokers. The disease, however, commonly occurs in non-smokers and the world-wide prevalence of this disease is quite unrelated to smoking habits. Smoking probably plays little or no part in causing gastric and duodenal ulcers but it does delay their healing and thus increases the risk of prolonged ill health and serious complications resulting from them. Death-rates from ulcers are higher in smokers of all kinds than in non-smokers.

SOME OTHER EFFECTS OF SMOKING

Smokers have been shown to be more *prone to accident* at work than non-smokers, but this does not imply a seriou hazard for the death-rate from accidents of all kinds ha not been found to be higher than in non-smokers in the prospective studies that have been made. Smokers are by nature rather less dependable in type than non-smokers and carelessness with cigarettes causes many fires in homes and factories every year. The paraphernalia of smoking has been found at the sites of explosions in coal mines which have caused loss of life and injury. It seems that some smokers are so addicted to the habit that they will risk their own lives and those of their fellow workers to satisfy their craving despite its prohibition in coal mines.

Most athletes abstain from smoking during training because of the widespread belief that it is '*bad for the wind*' but it is very difficult to test this belief. To do so would require that non-smoking athletes should be tested and then persuaded to smoke for various periods of time before being tested again, and smoking athletes would have to be tested and then give up the habit before being tested again. One such study has been made on only thirteen subjects. Five of these thirteen performed less well when smoking. Probably smoking impairs athletic performance in some but not all people. It also has been shown to cause an immediate increase in resistance to air-flow in the lungs of some subjects. Perhaps it is these who are adversely affected, for the increased resistance would make it more difficult for them to breathe.

One curious effect of smoking is on the *birth weight of babies* whose mothers smoke during pregnancy. This is on the average less than that of babies born to mothers who have not smoked. The reason for this is not understood.

Like all the other observations on the apparent effects of smoking it could be a chance association, due to mothers with a tendency to have small babies also having a tendency to smoke during pregnancy. But it has been suggested that nicotine may affect the blood supply to the placenta and thus affect the nutrition of the baby. The fact that the babies of smoking mothers are underweight does not appear to be of any great clinical importance; there is no difference in the frequency of complications of pregnancy and labour between smokers and non-smokers, nor are the babies of smoking mothers more often malformed. Indeed, because the babies are smaller the labour of smoking mothers may be, if anything, rather easier. In one investigation the proportion of underweight babies appeared to bear a closer relationship to the smoking habits of the fathers than to the smoking habits of the mothers. This is a remarkable observation which is quite beyond explanation. It is difficult to see how it could be due to cause and effect and it underlines the fact that an association between smoking and some disease or medical abnormality does not necessarily mean that smoking is its cause.

THE PROS AND CONS OF SMOKING

It needs no special inquiry to establish that smoking is pleasurable to many people, but it is worth inquiring what sort of people adopt the habit, why they start, and what it is in smoking to which they become so attached.

Several studies of the psychological make-up of smokers of various kinds and of non-smokers have been made in America and in this country. It has been found that cigarette smokers are more extraverted than non-smokers, while pipe smokers are more introverted even than non-smokers. Heavy smokers tend to be of a restless, ardent, and energetic personality; the non-smokers steadier, more dependable, and quieter. Cigarette smokers change their jobs and move house more often than non-smokers. Heavy smokers in one American study reported more neurotic symptoms and signs of anxiety than moderate smokers.

Studies of British and American schoolchildren have revealed very little about the reasons why they start smoking. It is not surprising to find that the children of smokers smoke more often than the children of non-smokers. More intelligent children smoke less than the less intelligent. The reason given by schoolboys and girls for their first smoke is usually that they wanted to satisfy their curiosity, that they wished to feel grown-up, or simply that someone offered them a cigarette. It is widely thought that starting to smoke is regarded as a sign of emancipation from the restrictions of childhood. The reasons why smoking so soon becomes a persistent habit are also obscure. The various manipulations of smoking certainly provide some pleasure or even relief from tension as may a wide variety of gesticulations or facial expressions, such as blinking or twitching the face, but no smoker enjoys an unlit cigarette or pipe. The smoke itself is important. It is unlikely that the complex mixture of tars and other chemical substances that provide the flavour of the smoke are a basis of addiction, for there is an enormous variety of flavours to any one of which a smoker may become attached and amongst which he may readily change. It is much more likely that it is the nicotine which is absorbed from the smoke to which the smoker becomes addicted. Little research has hitherto been done on this problem but it has been reported that injections of nicotine may relieve the desire for a cigarette in a heavy smoker. Nicotine is a nerve poison in large doses but in the small doses absorbed by a smoker it may be a nerve stimulant, and a possible pharmacological mechanism by which stimulation of the brain may occur has been suggested. It is extremely difficult to study claims that smoking produces a sense of relaxation in leisure or assists in concentration during work. The difference between smokers and non-smokers in many psychological respects means that differences in their average intellectual performance cannot be directly compared. Tests of heavy smokers after deprivation or of non-smokers after heavy smoking must inevitably be confused by the wide variety of mental and physical disturbances that such abrupt changes would produce.

Clinical experience suggests that a large proportion – perhaps as much as a third – of moderate or heavy smokers find it quite easy to stop once they are convinced of the need. These smokers do not seem to be really addicted and suffer little or no pangs of deprivation. They may be described as pure habit smokers. The remainder do appear to be really addicted and suffer acute sensations of restlessness and irritability when deprived of tobacco, symptoms which can be rapidly assuaged by a smoke. The symptoms of deprivation do not usually last long in this acute form, but a longing for tobacco, especially at times of stress, may persist for months or years.

Many people gain weight when they stop smoking. This is simply because they eat more. Smoking depresses appetite and instead of his cigarette after a meal an ex-smoker may nibble at an extra piece of bread or biscuit. The gain in weight is usually temporary and is easily reversed by deliberate control of the amount eaten. It is sometimes claimed by advocates of smoking that the risk of obesity (for in men, at least, mortality rates increase steadily with increasing weight above the normal range) is greater than the risk of continuing to smoke; but this is not true. All the prospective studies have shown a lower overall mortality, from all causes, in men who have stopped smoking than in those who continue to smoke.

THE RISKS OF SMOKING

The really important question to which any smoker or intending smoker needs an answer is how great is the risk, for the pleasures are quite obvious.

So far as British men are concerned the investigation of doctors' mortality rates in relation to smoking carried out by Doll and Hill provide the most relevant information. Table 1, extracted from the Royal College of Physicians' Report on Smoking and Health presents the essential figures. It will be seen that the difference between smokers and non-smokers is much greater at younger than at older ages. There are so many causes of death in old age that the additional risk of smoking is relatively small, but between the ages of thirty-five and forty-four smokers of twenty-five or more cigarettes a day have four times the mortality of non-smokers. The risk is shown in Table 2 as the fractional risk that the individual man has of dying within each of the ten-year periods between the ages of thirty-five and seventy-four.

Table 1. Death-rates from all causes per 1,000 per year.

Age	Non-smokers	Smokers of:		
		1–14/day	15–24/day	25 + /day
35–44	1·1	1·56	1·55	4·41
45–54	3·7	5·56	7·18	10·19
55–64	12·0	17·69	20·37	25·57
65–74	31·7	47·10	42·09	59·82

The significance of these figures may be considered in terms of a lottery, supposing that for each ten-year period the man has to draw from a box containing one black ball among a number of white ones. If he draws the black ball he dies in the next ten years. The ratios in the table show that for a non-smoker aged thirty-five there is only one black ball among ninety white ones for the next ten years, but there

Table 2. Fractional risk of dying from all causes in decades from age thirty-five to age seventy-four.

Decade	Non-smokers	Smokers of:		
		1–14/day	15–24/day	25 + /day
35–44	1 in 90	1 in 64	1 in 65	1 in 23
45–54	1 in 27	1 in 18	1 in 14	1 in 10
55–64	1 in 8	1 in 6	1 in 5	1 in 4
65–74	1 in 3	1 in 2	1 in 2	1 in 2

is one among only twenty-three for the heavy smoker. So far as attaining the usual age of retirement is concerned it will be seen that a man aged thirty-five has a fifteen-per-cent chance of dying before sixty-five (or eighty-five-per-cent chance of surviving) whereas a heavy smoker has twice the chance of dying, that is thirty-three-per-cent (or a sixty-seven-per-cent chance of surviving). See Table 3.

Table 3. Percentage of men aged thirty-five who may expect to die before the age of sixty-five.

Non-smokers	15
Smokers of 1–14/day	22
Smokers of 15–24/day	25
Smokers of 25/day or more	33

It is most important to realize that these figures do not imply that if the heavy smokers had not smoked they would have attained the figures shown by the non-smokers. Not all the difference between smokers and non-smokers is necessarily due to smoking. There are many psychological and other differences between smokers and non-smokers and these may affect mortality rates. The figures in the table represent the *maximum possible risk* of smoking for a professional man in this country. For the working class the risks are greater, for bronchitis, which is a smokers' disease, has five times the mortality among working men than it has among the professional classes. The fact that all surveys have shown a reduced mortality in men who have given up smoking certainly suggests that foresaking the habit may reduce the risk, but even this is not certain, for those smokers who are liable to give up the habit may have a smaller innate liability to disease than those who are more heavily addicted.

So far as the community is concerned we need to look at the number of deaths occurring each year from diseases which are at least partly caused by smoking. Taking men between the ages of thirty and sixty-four, in their active working lives, lung cancer kills 10,000 in England and Wales. At least eighty per cent or 8,000 of these deaths are probably due to smoking cigarettes. Bronchitis kills 6,000. Very few of these deaths would have occurred if none of the patients had smoked. Coronary heart disease kills 20,000 but it is impossible to say to how many of these deaths smoking contributed. A conservative estimate might be one-tenth, say 2,000. The number of deaths from gastric and duodenal ulcer is only about 1,000 and a relatively small proportion of these can be attributed to smoking. The total toll of deaths in men of working age is therefore about 16,000 per annum (more than twice the number of deaths due to road accidents at all ages), and about ten per cent of these deaths occur before the age of fifty. It is sad to think of 1,600 unnecessary funerals of men under the age of fifty every year (forty-four every day) due to cigarette smoking, and we must not forget that every day there are nine times as many funerals of men aged fifty to sixty-four who would not have died if they had not smoked.

WHAT NEEDS TO BE DONE?

To save life and preserve health, is it necessary that cigarette smoking should be proscribed? Is there nothing else that can be done more readily and effectively?

Prevention of air pollution is the measure chiefly advocated by those most interested in promoting cigarette smoking – the tobacco manufacturers. There is no doubt at all of the adverse effects of air pollution on health. Moreover, the incidence of the more important cigarette diseases – lung cancer and bronchitis – is certainly promoted by air pollution. Nevertheless, in countries such as Finland with less air pollution than could possibly be achieved in our industrialized country within the foreseeable future, cigarette consumption and lung-cancer death-rates are almost as high as ours, and even in the least polluted countries cigarette smokers have a much higher incidence of this disease and of bronchitis than non-smokers. Prevention of air pollution is most desirable but it cannot provide complete protection against the dangers of cigarette smoking.

It is notable that the great majority of cigarette smokers enjoy the habit without impairment or shortening of life. Is it really necessary to deny them their pleasure in order to save a minority of smokers from disability and premature death? If we could *detect the susceptible people* our preventive measures could be concentrated on them without interfering with the others. At present, unfortunately, we know of no way by which we could identify these susceptibles. Those who already have arterial disease or coronary heart disease or gastric ulcer must certainly eschew smoking, but more than this is needed. Undoubtedly smokers who have a smoker's cough are those most prone to bronchitis, and there is some evidence that these coughers may also be more susceptible to lung cancer. But unfortunately many patients with lung cancer deny any previous cough and since nearly half of all cigarette smokers have a cough, forbidding smoking to all coughers would be a fairly Draconian measure. We need to find out whether there are any other ways in which those smokers at special risk could be identified. To investigate this we would have to carry out a survey of symptoms, of psychological and other characteristics, and of smoking habits in a large population – probably at least 50,000 in number, who would then be followed in subsequent years to see which of them became ill and died and of what causes. This would be a vast and difficult undertaking but it should be done.

The possibility of *removing the harmful substances* from the smoke has been carefully investigated. Tobacco smoke consists of a cloud of minute particles (ten to forty millionths of an inch in diameter) all of which probably have the same chemical composition, so it is difficult to see how to filter out from these droplets any particular harmful substances such as nicotine or tarry material containing carcinogenic substances. However, some of the irritant substances and co-carcinogens in the smoke exist in a gaseous form and it is possible to filter some of them out selectively. Filters could, of course, be made which would retain all the smoke, but such a filter would remove all the pleasure from smoking and would not be acceptable. Theoretically, it would seem that filters which remove co-carcinogens and some of the tar should reduce the risks of smoking. At present there is no way by which the smoker can tell, if he chooses a filter-tipped cigarette, what sort of efficiency this filter has. Nor can any guarantee be given that a cigarette, even with an efficient filter, would be safer than an unfiltered cigarette. To prove this it would be necessary to observe large numbers of smokers who smoked such cigarettes exclusively while others continued with unfiltered brands. In the course of ten or twenty years it would be possible to discover whether the incidence of the disease was different in the two groups.

It is also possible to modify the tobacco itself so that the cigarettes produce a smoke with a reduced tar and nicotine content. Again it would be difficult and would take a long time to discover whether smoking such cigarettes carried a smaller risk than smoking ordinary cigarettes. The immediate irritant effect of filtered cigarettes or cigarettes made with modified tobaccos could be tested by observing their effect on smoker's cough. This is an investigation which needs to be done.

The unburnt part of the cigarette acts as a filter and some of the smoke from the first half of the cigarette is condensed in the second half. When the second half is burnt the deposit within it is redistilled so that the smoke of the second half of the cigarette contains a higher concentration of harmful materials than the first. If cigarette smokers could be persuaded to stub out their cigarettes before the second half was burnt their risk would almost certainly be reduced (and the interests of the tobacco manufacturers would be enhanced). It is difficult to see how such a change of habit could be brought about without a great reduction in the cost of cigarettes, and even then the total numbers of cigarettes each smoker consumed would probably be increased until the risk had returned to its original level.

Perhaps the most likely change that could be both satisfying to smokers and which would reduce the risk would be to persuade them to change from smoking cigarettes to smoking pipes and cigars. A change of this kind might be encouraged by a change in the taxation of tobaccos, reducing that on pipe and cigar tobaccos and increasing the tax on cigarette tobaccos. Such a change of habit would certainly greatly reduce the risk, but there are many that think that the smell of pipe and cigar smoke is so unpleasant that the aesthetic harm would scarcely justify the benefit to health!

Improvements in medical treatment do not seem likely to bring much help to those who damage their lungs by smoking. At the time of diagnosis lung cancer has already spread beyond the lungs and is thus incurable in four out of five cases. In those in whom there is no sign of spread, cure may be achieved by a surgeon removing the affected lung or part of it, but only one out of every twenty cases at the time of diagnosis can hope to live as long as five years. Most live for less than a year. At any time medical science may, of course, discover some new and revolutionary way of arresting the violent growth and spread of cancer throughout the body, but there is no sign of any such discovery at the moment in relation to lung cancer.

Antibiotics can help to shorten attacks of acute bronchitis but only slight relief can be given for the shortness of breath that is so distressing to the established case of chronic bronchitis. The effect of giving up cigarettes relatively early, however, is often quite dramatic and beneficial.

So the only sure defence against the hazards of smoking cigarettes is not to smoke them. At present social custom and the pressure of skilled and extensive advertising encourage a steady increase in this dangerous habit. Many doctors, who every day see the tragic effects of cigarette smoking in their patients, are giving up smoking cigarettes. If only the general population in this country could be brought to face the facts, as doctors have, they might be persuaded to act with good sense and caution and to stop smoking. If they did this a vast access of health would be achieved for them and for future generations.

THE ECONOMIC EFFECTS

Harvey Cole

THE British public spends about 1s. 6d. in every pound of
its income on tobacco. The effect of this on the national
economy is in many respects much slighter than the bare
figures might suggest. Direct employment in the tobacco
industry is not large, and, even on the distribution side,
the number of people directly deriving a livelihood from
tobacco is only moderate. However, trade in cigarettes,
which is relatively inexpensive to run, provides the marginal
profit which keeps a large number of small traders in business, even though the actual profits on tobacco goods are
themselves slender.

The impact of the tobacco industry on the national revenue is very much greater: duties on tobacco now account
for nearly twenty per cent of the Government's annual income.

On the international economic scene the importance of
Britain as a customer for tobacco is considerable: any withdrawal from this position would affect the prices received
by tobacco producers in several countries on a sufficiently
substantial scale to reduce local living standards to an ap-
preciable extent.

While the Government derives a large income from
tobacco, there is also a large debit balance to be recorded
in the shape of accelerated death and aggravated illnesses
which seem to be attributable to the smoking habit. This
is also reflected in a loss of output exceeding by a large
margin that lost through strikes.

Early in the seventeenth century, after James I had raised the tax on tobacco from Elizabeth's 2d. per lb. to a savage 6s. 10d., it used to change hands at more than the price of silver. John Aubrey reports of that period: 'I have heard some of the old yeomen neighbours say that when they went to Malmesbury or Chippenham market, they culled out their biggest shillings to lay in the scales against the tobacco.'

This year the British public will spend something like £1,250 million on tobacco, and this will buy them around 280 million lb. of the processed plant. Silver now commands about £6 15s. per lb. so that tobacco, at £4 10s., is still two-thirds as valuable today as the precious metal.

The Government's Survey of Family Expenditure, carried out in 1961, showed that the country's households spent an average of 20s. 6d. a week on tobacco, while pensioners' homes could manage only 4s. 11d. Impressive as the average figure may seem, it understates reality: as the Survey primly records of its findings, 'the results are not adjusted to take account of the under-recording of expenditure on alcoholic drink, tobacco, meals out, chocolates, sweets, and ice-cream, which is a feature of surveys of this kind'. In the case of tobacco the degree of understatement is of the order of one-third.

In 1961 total consumer expenditure on tobacco amounted to £1,218 million, which was a jump of £283 million (or about thirty per cent) on the level only five years earlier. Of course, the ever-increasing appetite of the Chancellor of the Exchequer played a part in the rise: the 1960 Budget raised the duty levied on tobacco to a record of 64s. 4d. per lb. and this was effectively boosted to well over 70s. by the ten-per-cent surcharge on most indirect taxes introduced in July 1961 by Mr Selwyn Lloyd. Altogether, price increases, including those imposed by the manufacturers, amounted to fifteen per cent over the five years between 1956 and 1961, so that the actual quantities consumed went up by thirteen per cent, or a little more than two per cent annually.

In 1961 tobacco actually accounted for a full seven per cent of all consumer spending (it is allowed a weighting of eight per cent in the compilation of the official index of retail prices) and took a larger slice of each pound spent than did fuel and light, furniture and floor coverings combined. About 120,000 million cigarettes were smoked, or nearly 2,400 for every man, woman, and child in the country. The twenty-one million smokers thus had an average ration of getting on for 6,000, the seventy-five per cent of men who smoke getting through about nineteen a day, while the fifty per cent of women who now smoke (the highest proportion yet recorded) each managed ten a day on average. Incidentally, while only two women smoke for every three men, and they smoke only half as heavily, the gap has been narrowing rapidly in recent years, and it is thought that since the outbreak of war in 1939 about fifty-six per cent of the increase in cigarette consumption is attributable to women.

Other kinds of tobacco have not flourished on the same scale as the cigarette. Pipe smoking has declined and the tobacco used in this way is now less than half the pre-war figure. There has been a drop of as much as a third even since 1950, and sales of pipe tobacco are now barely larger than the consumption of tobacco in cigarettes which people roll for themselves. Little more than a million men are now exclusively faithful to a pipe in their smoking habits, and they, together with the occasional devotees of the pipe, spend barely six per cent of all money that goes on tobacco.

Cigars, although long past their heyday, have made something of a recovery in the last ten years. This year will see about eight cigars smoked per adult male (compared with over 7,000 cigarettes), but this is an improvement of a half since 1950, when consumption of tobacco for cigars was under two million lb. as against five million lb. in 1907 when cigarettes had already started to oust the larger product.

Thus, the cigarette in its various forms now accounts for well over ninety per cent of all tobacco consumed in this country, and this dominance is reflected in the list of brand names published in one of the industry's year books. This devotes over fifty closely printed columns, spread over seventeen pages, to a list of brands on the market – and follows it by a further nineteen columns of fancy goods associated with smoking, making a total of nearly 4,000 different lines available to the eager smoker in search of variety.

For an industry whose products absorb so much of the nation's spending, tobacco employs surprisingly few people, and this impression remains even when allowance is made for the fact that getting on for ninety per cent of the manufacturers' gross income is now absorbed by the duty.

Rather fewer than 40,000 people work in the tobacco manufacturing industry itself, and the Player's and Wills's cigarette factories of the Imperial Tobacco Company, situated at Nottingham and Bristol respectively, account for practically half the total.

The distribution of the industry's labour force among the various regions of the country clearly reflects this dominance. In April 1962 the employment pattern was as follows in Table 4.

At the same date unemployment in Nottingham amounted to 4,423, or 1·9 per cent of the labour force (the same proportion as in the country as a whole) whereas in Bristol unemployment was 3,473 or only 1·4 per cent. Should the tobacco industry be closed down overnight, these cities would find their unemployment rates about trebled, although the proportion of local jobs made up by the industry is only about five per cent.

Table 4.

Midlands	8,350
South-west	8,440
London, South-east	6,270
North-west	7,540
East, South	4,720
North	1,380
Scotland	2,660
Wales	420

The tobacco industry offers a combination of above-average earnings and slightly longer hours than in manufacturing as a whole. In April 1962 the rates and hours for tobacco workers compared with the figures for all manufacturing industries were as shown in Table 5.

Table 5.

	Tobacco		All Industries	
	Wages	Hours (Weekly)	Wages	Hours (Weekly)
Men	£15 14 2	44·7	£15 12 10	47·3
Youths	£8 9 4	43·0	£7 1 3	43·5
Women	£9 4 7	41·2	£7 17 2	39·6
(part-time)	£4 9 4	21·5	£4 1 0	21·7
Girls	£6 15 0	41·0	£5 4 6	40·4

Males thus actually worked a shorter than average week, and this was reflected in the smaller margin by which their earnings exceeded those paid in other industries. Over all, hourly rates average ten per cent above the general run in industry.

The industry's labour force is made up roughly of thirty-four per cent men, two per cent youths, forty-five per cent full-time women, with ten per cent part-time, and nine per cent girls. The total weekly wage-bill in October 1961 would have been about £400,000, or an annual rate of £20 million. This figure is actually less than the Imperial Tobacco Company's profits in 1951, and confirms the relative unimportance of labour in tobacco manufacturing costs, as well as the industry's minor role in total employment: out of just under nine million people in manufacturing, tobacco accounts for no more than 0·45 per cent.

The predominance of Imperial Tobacco is less than it has been: in 1959 it accounted for just over sixty-three per cent of all tobacco sales, while its nearest rival, Gallahers, stood at under thirty per cent. However, at the height of its power, in 1947, Imperial had over seventy-eight per cent of the industry's turnover, and more than eighty-one per cent of sales of cigarettes alone.

Manufacturers other than Imperial and Gallaher are reduced to under seven per cent of the total. As Imperial's arguments against implementing of the recommendation of the Monopolies Commission that it should be divested of its forty-two-per-cent shareholding in its main rival seem to have carried weight with the President of the Board of Trade, any picture of the industry must inevitably be a portrait most of whose features bear an uncanny resemblance to those of Imperial itself. Indeed, quite apart from its substantial stake in Gallaher, Imperial has extended tentacles into most other fields connected with tobacco: it has a controlling interest in Finlays, the multiple retail tobacconists; a large holding in British-American Tobacco, which operates overseas; and a twenty-five-per-cent stake in Molins, which dominates the manufacture of cigarette-making and packaging machinery. A further twenty-five per cent of the voting control of Molins, which is based on only £17,160 in Ordinary shares out of a total issued capital of

£1,680,000, is vested in British-American Tobacco. Imperial also has several other less important investments in tobacco making and distribution, including control of Ardath and a holding in Robert Sinclair the tobacconists.

One example of the way in which this widespread control operates may be mentioned. Molins produces over fifty per cent by value of all tobacco-making machinery made in this country, as well as enjoying rights to manufacture under licence from American concerns. By virtue of the twin facts of its own dominant position as a customer and as a shareholder, Imperial was able to reach an agreement with Molins whereby Imperial has the right to sixty days' exclusive use of the prototype of any new machine produced by Molins, with subsequent priority in delivery, before other manufacturers' orders can be met. In this way Imperial was able to ensure that its own filter-tip cigarettes came on to the market ahead of any of its competitors' brands in 1949, and it secured a similar advantage in bringing out the new flip-top type packets before the other manufacturers.

In 1959 Imperial's total sales amounted to £592 million. Of this the cost of tobacco in leaf accounted for 7·4 per cent; manufacturing expenses for 5·7 per cent, and gross profits for 3·6 per cent. The balance, or 83·3 per cent, was represented by the duty levied on the tobacco by the Government. Sales net of duty thus amounted to barely £100 million, so that, related to this figure, profits were about twenty-one per cent. It must of course be remembered that tobacco manufacturers have to keep substantial sums locked up in the financing of their tobacco stocks, although this can be minimized by the use of bonded warehouses.

By contrast with the position in many other industries, there is little evidence of Imperial's monopolistic position resulting in its economic efficiency lagging behind. The investigation by the Monopolies Commission, which re-ported in 1961, found that the time taken to produce a million standard cigarettes by the various firms varied from 178 man-hours to 345, and that it was the Wills's and Player's factories which recorded the lowest figures.

It is of course the case that the company has access to new machinery on favourable terms as it becomes avail-able, and that it operates on a larger scale than its competitors, with the exception of Gallaher, but the com-paratively high level of productive efficiency remains, and is reflected in a substantially higher figure of net output per worker employed in tobacco than in the general run of other industries. In purely economic terms, a redeployment of the tobacco industry's labour force into other jobs is likely to reduce the overall performance of British industry rather than improve it.

The very substantial operating margins shown by the manufacturing end of the tobacco industry are not matched by similar rates of profit in distribution. The 1957 Census of Distribution covered outlets responsible for sales of tobacco goods worth £637 million out of an estimated total spent across the counter by consumers of £981 mil-lion in that year. The bulk of the difference between these figures is accounted for by public houses, hotels, restaur-ants, etc.

Of the £637 million, well over half, or £388 million, came from sales by the general group of confectioners, newsagents, and tobacconists. Tobacco in fact accounted for about fifty-five per cent of the total turnover of this group of shops, which stood at £692 million in 1957.

It so happens that this category of shop showed one of the lowest rates of gross margin on turnover of all the sections analysed in the Census of Distribution. The figure stood at 14·9 per cent, against an average for all retail outlets of 22·3 per cent. Shops which were part of an organization with ten or more branches showed rather better results, with gross margins of 17·7 per cent, whereas their smaller colleagues could not do better than an average of 14·6 per cent.

These figures compare with margins well in excess of thirty per cent for the majority of other non-food shops such as bookshops, china and glass shops, and jewellers. Cigarettes and tobacco, making up over half his turnover, actually give smaller margins than the confectioner or newsagent-cum-tobacconist achieves on his total business, if the margins quoted by Imperial to the Monopolies Commission are any guide to the trade as a whole.

It was then stated that the margins allowed to retailers on cigarettes varied between 10·4 and 11·4 per cent, while those on tobacco were fractionally lower.

There is only one category of shop which showed lower gross margins than tobacconists at the time of the 1957 Census, and this was 'grocers and provision merchants', whose returns averaged 14·4 per cent. Strangely enough, though the coincidence bears no sinister significance, this group of shops follows the newsagent/confectioners as the second most substantial retail outlet for tobacco, selling £132-million-worth in 1957, or over twenty per cent of all sales of this kind, and a third as much as the confectionery/ newsagent group.

However, while tobacco made up over half of the former shops' total turnover, it accounted for a mere eight and a half per cent of the total of grocers' sales of all kinds, amounting to £1,556 million.

Cigarettes and tobacco are of small, but varying, significance to other retail traders. Other food shops sold nearly £19-million-worth in 1957, constituting less than one and a half per cent of their combined turnover of £1,331 million. For some reason greengrocers sold the most, with £3·6 million, followed by bakers with £1·5 million, while dairymen had sales worth £0·6 million.

Shops whose main business is in clothing sold £0·3-million-worth of cigarettes, while hardware shops recorded sales of £0·4 million, half of it by ironmongers.

Booksellers disposed of £1·4 million, about one and a half per cent of their turnover – a proportion reached by greengrocers alone of the other groups mentioned. Jewellers did about as well with tobacco sales of £1·9 million, while the chemists' figure of £1·6 was well under one per cent. General, department, and variety stores sold almost £10 million between them, but this was also less than one per cent of their combined turnover.

The other principal retail outlet for tobacco is of course the off-licence (the pub itself not being classified as retail trade) and in 1957 off-licences sold £9·3 million worth of cigarettes and tobacco out of a total turnover of £112 million – about eight per cent.

It follows from these figures that trade in tobacco is of major importance only to the confectioners and newsagents, although grocers and off-licensees find it a useful secondary source of business.

Without cigarettes many thousands of small shops would clearly find it impossible to stay in business, even though the margins on them are substantially below those on the other goods they handle.

In 1957 there were 77,440 confectioners, newsagents, and tobacconists, and, while no precise figures are available, it is clear that the vast majority of them dealt in cigarettes. This total was some 2,800 higher than in 1950, so that today there could be almost 80,000 such shops. Most of them are small and independent: in 1957 those which belonged to groups controlling ten or more outlets numbered no more than 6,361, so that somewhere between 50,000 and 60,000 are predominantly the one-man business type of shop providing a wide range of goods for inhabitants of the immediate neighbourhood – and often these days supplementing their service by remaining open for extended hours. These shops make up about ten per cent of all retail outlets, and while they do very much less than ten per cent of the country's business (in fact about five per cent of total retail trade) they clearly perform a valuable function not entirely to be measured by their economic efficiency. Their loss would cause considerable dislocation and hardship, necessitating among other things new systems for the distribution of newspapers, sweets, and ice-cream that could considerably increase the cost of these goods, not least because the organizations that would come in would probably demand a higher return than is acceptable to the retired or semi-retired trader who often runs a tobacconist's shop now for a low return on his own labour.

In 1957 over 285,000 people were employed in confectioners, newsagents, and tobacconists. This compares with a total of just under two million in retail distribution at that time, of whom about sixty per cent were women. Of the total just over a quarter, or 72,300 were working proprietors and unpaid helpers. There were 57,000 full-time employees, three quarters of them female, and 134,000 part-time workers, of whom two-thirds were male. Between them they transacted sales totalling £700 million, of which branches of concerns with ten or more shops accounted for £80 million. Thus, about 130,000 people are concerned directly and full-time with this sector of the retail trade in tobacco, and would have to find other work or an alternative outlet in which to invest their savings if for some reason cigarettes and tobacco disappeared. The part-time workers would mostly either not look for other jobs or would find another source of pocket money fairly easily.

The wages paid in these shops totalled £27·8 million in 1957, and are probably over £33 million this year. This compares with £717 million paid out in wages in all retail establishments in 1957, so that this group of shops accounts for about four per cent of retail wages. In most other retail outlets the cost of handling and selling tobacco is clearly marginal, and the proportion of the wages bill attributed to this activity must be small: employment would be little different if occasional sales of cigarettes were not made, whereas in the confectionery and newsagents' group the absence of tobacco sales would make it difficult, if not impossible in many cases, to continue in business at all, so that the proportion of wages attributable to tobacco sales must be substantial.

All in all, payments for employment in retailing tobacco can be put at around £50 million, which would include the cost of distributing goods from the manufacturers to the shops. In terms of the *full-time* labour which might be displaced by a prohibition on tobacco, this might include all told 100,000 people, of whom a third might be expected to retire or not seek further jobs.

Mention should be made here of the bonus schemes operated by the tobacco companies, notably Imperial, which were designed to secure the best possible display of their goods in retailers' windows and shops. Imperial had two schemes, under one of which they undertook to provide shopkeepers with new facia boards in return for having their own brands displayed so as to take up seventy-five per cent of the window space, and to have centre spaces in windows reserved for them. The other, more widespread scheme ensured for Imperial a fully proportionate share of display space in relation to their share of the market. Gallaher ran similar schemes on a more or less *ad hoc* basis when a campaign was being mounted in a particular area, but the smaller firms found it difficult to compete on this front and had to rely for their displays on the shopkeeper's goodwill. Imperial gave an undertaking to wind their scheme up after 31 October 1962.

In 1959 there were just over 100,000 participants entitled to share in the Imperial bonus scheme. The bonus is related to the proportion of the shareholders' dividend arising from net sales in the home market, and in 1959 amounted to a further 0·68 per cent paid to retailers and wholesalers alike. This represented about a five-per-cent bonus to retailers (but as much as twenty-two per cent to wholesalers whose normal discounts are below three per cent). The bonus makes a useful Christmas present for the shopkeeper (public house tills bulge with the encashed cheques on Christmas Eve) but little more. In 1959 25,000 of the recipients got less than £5, and a further 60,000 qualified for between £5 and £25 while only 450 had sufficient turnover for the bonus to be worth more than £1,000 to them.

The real importance of the tobacco industry to the country's industrial and commercial structure is thus considerably smaller than a first consideration of the expenditure on cigarettes might suggest. Less than one worker out of every 200 in manufacturing industry is directly employed in tobacco manufacturing, and the inclusion of those in machinery making and other fringe activities such as lighters, pipes, and accessories, and the matches used by smokers (about 2,000 million boxes a year), would not make much difference. On the distribution side about one worker in twenty in the retail trade would be displaced without tobacco, but many would not seek new jobs. The main impact here would be the disappearance of many thousands of small shops and probably a more expensive structure of distribution for newspapers and confectionery.

In terms of the incomes concerned, only about £50 million to £60 million in all is involved, or about two per cent of the national income, and even in the areas where tobacco manufacture is heavily concentrated, its disappearance would not create any major problems provided that this did not simply happen overnight.

The marginal importance of tobacco in production and distribution is not paralleled where advertising is concerned. Tobacco advertising has risen sharply since 1955, and now accounts for a larger proportion of all advertising expenditure than at any time in the past. Advertisers have been reconsidering their tactics and the type of appeal to adopt since the publication of the Royal College of Physicians' Report on Smoking and Health, but it is unlikely that there will be any serious reduction in the actual volume of expenditure, whatever the changes in emphasis, unless there is direct intervention by the Government.

The industry's reaction to suggestions that its advertising expenditure was too lavish, made by the Royal College, elicited an interesting reply, which appears in the Appendix to the Report. There it was stated:

Press and television advertising expenditure on tobacco goods in the U.K. in 1959 was 0·52 per cent of retail expenditure on those goods whereas press and television advertising expenditure on all consumer goods and services was 0·87 per cent of retail expenditure on all consumer goods and services. Press and television advertising expenditure on tobacco goods could thus be increased two-thirds without exceeding the proportion that press and television advertising expenditure on consumer goods and services generally bears to public expenditure on these goods and services.

This turgid and repetitious statement by the Tobacco Advisory Committee conceals a serious omission which invalidates the whole of the case it is trying to make. For, as the tobacco industry is so quick to point out on every other conceivable occasion, the price of cigarettes is made up as to nearly ninety per cent by tax, a far higher proportion than is borne by any other commodity or service. Indeed, the general level of taxes on other goods and services is less than ten per cent. If the whole of the tobacco manufacturer's gross receipts were spent on advertising, he could still not achieve a higher figure than fifteen per cent of his sales. The proper comparison is of course to set advertising expenditure against turnover net of duty, and on this basis the tobacco industry's figure is about 2·2 per cent against less than one per cent for all other goods and services. Thus, in 1959 the tobacco industry advertised twice as heavily as the average, and the discrepancy increased further in 1960, a fact to which the Tobacco Advisory Committee does not refer.

Heavy advertising is of course no proof of sin, but playing down the fact of its existence certainly suggests a troubled conscience.

In the last few years there has been a very rapid rise in the money spent on advertising tobacco. Table 6 shows the expenditure on the two main forms of advertising, Press display and television.

In 1960 tobacco advertising made up over two per cent of all advertising in the press, a slightly higher proportion than in the preceding years. However, the advance on television went on at an even greater rate, so that from less than half the press figure in 1957 television moved ahead in 1959, and has since built up a very substantial lead. In 1960 tobacco made up nearly six per cent of all advertising on television. This pattern continued in 1961, but there are signs of a change since then.

Advertising by the tobacco industry does not end with

the press and television however. To the £9 million or so
spent on these media in 1961 must be added expenditure
on posters and advertising outdoors in other forms. Despite
the competition of television, these outlets still attract a
great deal of money, and the Advertising Inquiry Council
estimates that they absorbed over £2·5 million in 1960.

Table 6.

	(£ million)	
	Press	Television
1954	1·3	—
1955	1·7	
1956	2·2	
1957	2·6	1·1
1958	2·8	
1959	2·7	3·0
1960	3·8	4·5
1961	3·8	5·3

In addition there is expenditure on window-dressing
and display which must properly be regarded as part of the
manufacturers' promotion budget. This too is thought to
be running at an annual rate of about £2.5 million.

Gift-coupon schemes are a form of promotion less
directly connected with advertising, but not completely
divorced from it. This is not now a widespread form of
activity, being confined to the brands Kensitas, Ardath, and
Embassy. There is not in fact much scope for coupon
trading with cigarettes, a fact which again reflects the high
level of duty. It was estimated in 1957 that the exchange
value of coupons in a packet of twenty cigarettes then costing 3s. 10d. was 2½d. although the cost to the manufacturer
of the goods being used as gifts was probably no more than
1¼d. This still amounted to five per cent of the retail price,

and to as much as a quarter of the manufacturer's own selling price after deducting the duty. Even allowing for the fact that a high proportion of the coupons issued are never presented for redemption, this can be an expensive method of promotion: a twenty-per-cent redemption rate would still absorb five per cent of the manufacturer's return and make it more expensive than other forms of advertising unless an unusually high rate of attraction of new customers were achieved. The cost of these schemes might be put at about £1 million a year at most.

All in all, therefore, the tobacco manufacturers are spending at the rate of £14 million to £15 million a year on advertising and allied types of publicity, and about three-quarters of the total is spent on press, television, and posters, making up about four per cent of the total spent on these media by all users. Clearly any major restriction of publicity for tobacco would cause some agonizing reappraisals on both sides of the advertising accounts, and most markedly where television is concerned. The elimination of so large a slice of existing business would probably include among its repercussions a raising of rates to other advertisers, so that, to this extent, tobacco advertisers might be said to be subsidizing other users to a perceptible degree. There is no reason, however, to think that the elimination of tobacco advertisements would have the effect of compelling an increase in the prices of newspapers and periodicals in general.

The Government is a very small advertiser where tobacco is concerned – a figure of £2,500 has been mentioned for the current muted campaign to draw attention to the dangers of smoking. But this is about the only small sum of money that can be discovered in connexion with the Government and tobacco. In the financial year 1960-1 the tax on tobacco raised over £825 million, and accounted for about a fifth of all the money raised by direct and indirect taxation. The addition of the ten-per-cent surcharge in July 1961, and the impact of the latest reports linking lung cancer and smoking, make it complex to estimate the Government's income from the duty for the current year, but it would be surprising if the 1962-3 receipts do not exceed the £900 million mark, more than enough to meet the combined Central Government expenditure on roads and health, or on education.

This dependence of the Government on revenue from tobacco is the central economic fact about the commodity. In 1900 the duty was only 3s. a lb. and the revenue amounted to barely £10 million. By 1930 the rate was 8s. 10d. and the income derived from it was nearly £63 million, and on the eve of the outbreak of war in 1939 the rate of duty had been further increased to 11s. 6d. while revenue had exceeded £82 million. But never at any time during this period did the duty bear anything like the relation to total Government revenue that it does today: before the war it constituted about eight per cent of such receipts, so that its importance has multiplied nearly threefold.

But the tax on tobacco itself, which does not discriminate between the various uses to which unmanufactured tobacco may subsequently be put, does not exhaust the list of levies imposed by a grateful Government on the willing smoker.

Quite apart from the reasonable but not precisely identified sum raised each year by purchase tax on the various smokers' requisities and accessories, there is a specific tax imposed on mechanical lighters. In 1960-1 this brought in £868,000, made up of a Customs revenue of £187,000 on 537,000 imported lighters, and £681,000 by an Excise duty, whose existence will surprise most smokers, levied on nearly two and a half million home-made instruments.

A substantial proportion of the £12·68 million brought in by the tax on matches in the same period ought properly to be credited to the industrious smoker, and then there are the licences which have to be bought by those manufacturing or trading in tobacco. Manufacturers pay according to the quantity of tobacco they process: a mere beginner escapes with five guineas for his first year, but has to pay a surcharge if he manages to get through more than 20,000 lb. of tobacco. At the other end of the scale, a processor of more than 100,000 lb. has to foot the Government's bill to the large extent of £31 10s. Only about ninety licences are current, so that the revenue is not strongly fortified from this particular source.

Dealers must also be licensed, and there are currently about 430,000 licences in issue. These brought in £180,000 in 1960-1, but, sad to tell, will probably be less productive in future because of a change in the system. Formerly licences were issued annually at the strange price of 5s. 3d. (and occasional licences were available at the rate of 4d. a day). Now a licence costs £1 and is valid for three years to 31 December of the year following that of issue.

All these taxes and duties naturally pale besides the magnitude of the levy on the leaf itself, adding barely one per cent to its enormous yield. The manufacturers have to exercise great care to ensure that they do not pay even more than the heavy rate prescribed of just under 71s. a pound. This figure is based on tobacco with a moisture content of ten per cent. If the tobacco comes in wetter than this on arrival in this country, the importer simply has the pleasure of paying duty on plain water at a rate of over £35 a gallon. On the other hand, if the tobacco is drier and a moisture content of less than ten per cent is found in any part of a cask, the duty on that cask is recalculated at a higher rate. To eliminate this risk shippers normally allow a slight excess over the ten per cent, so that H.M. Customs effectively collects many millions of pounds each year on imported water from the United States, Greece, Turkey, India, Canada, Rhodesia, and elsewhere, although a preferential rate is allowed to the Commonwealth countries.

Clearly, the Government has the largest vested interest in the continued existence of the tobacco industry, and it is not at all easy to suggest how the prospective loss of revenue could be equitably made good if an income of £2·5 million a day had to be found from other sources. As about sixty per cent of all adults are smokers, and the proportion of those in employment who smoke is even higher, a tentative solution that might be acceptable if such a situation ever came about could be for the money required to be levied by a payroll tax. Alternatively, or additionally, the existing structure of purchase tax could be adapted to a flat-rate levy on most goods and services, designed to bring in rather more revenue than purchase tax.

Whatever the difficulties, it is clear enough that the tax revenue that would be forgone on cigarettes if smoking dies out or is prohibited could be replaced with a little imagination. Certainly, while the size of the income must act as a disincentive to the Civil Service mind, there is no inherent reason why the money required to run the country's affairs should not be found without resort to tobacco. Furthermore, as shown later, there would be substantial social savings that could reasonably be expected to follow from a disappearance of smoking, and these can be set against the current level of revenue, which would have the effect of reducing the sum to be found in substitution.

First, however, it is well to consider the importance of Britain's trade in tobacco to the economy of other countries, quite apart from our own balance of payments.

Until the middle of the last century smoking was confined to pipes and cigars. It is generally accepted to have been the Crimean War which introduced the cigarette to England, and until about the end of the nineteenth century the tobaccos used in English cigarettes were primarily of the Oriental types imported from Turkey and the Balkan countries. However, at about the turn of the century, cigarette smoking spread to wider circles, and to encourage this manufacturers turned to the milder flavoured tobaccos found in Virginia and other southern American states. There are cynics who say that the real reason for the change was that Virginian tobacco was found to be more addicting, but the more plausible explanation is, for once, the simpler one that the milder flavour offered the best chance of rapidly extending the market, particularly among women.

The rise of the cigarette led to a radical switch in the source of British supplies, with America playing a dominant role until an attempt was made to build up tobacco growing in various colonial territories, notably Rhodesia, between the wars, a policy which was given further impetus by the development of Imperial Preference.

Ironically enough, the preference for Virginia tobacco cost Britain dear immediately after the war when it was necessary for millions of scarce dollars to be allotted for the purchase of American tobacco to maintain supplies. Had British smokers had different tastes, our post-war problems would have been appreciably alleviated.

Commonwealth tobacco was slow in establishing its popularity, despite the introduction of a preferential rate of duty in 1919, when it was fixed at five-sixths of the full rate. Between 1925 and 1927 it was set at three-quarters of the full rate, giving an effective preference of twenty-five per cent. It was then changed to a fixed preference of 2s. 0½d. a pound, which of course effectively deteriorated

as a percentage protection as the rate of duty was itsel
raised to successively higher levels. During the war th
margin was further cut to 1s. 6½d. at which level it sti
remains. But, as the duty has risen from 11s. 6d. to nearl
71s. since 1939, the effective preference has dropped fror
twenty-one and a half per cent to no more than two and
half per cent. Nevertheless, the proportion of Common
wealth tobacco used in the British industry has been stead
ily stepped up until it now accounts for half of tota
consumption, whereas in the pre-war period the Unite
States was the dominant source of supply.

In recent years British imports of tobacco on the 'greer
basis (including the ten per cent moisture) have been run
ning at about 300 million lb. annually, equivalent to aroun
270 million lb. dry weight, out of total world tobacc
exports of 1,100 million lb. so that the country is respon
sible for nearly thirty per cent of trade in this commodit

World production of tobacco is approximately 6,00
million lb., of which nearly a sixth is grown in China. Th
United States, with a sixth of the acreage, produces a
much as thirty per cent of the total, reflecting the hig
yields secured by American tobacco growers. The Common
wealth has about a third of the total acreage, most of it i
India and Pakistan, and grows a fifth of the world cro
Yields in India and Pakistan are low. Rhodesia and N
asaland have between them about a fifth of the land plante
to tobacco in the Commonwealth, divided almost equall
between Southern Rhodesia on the one hand and Norther
Rhodesia and Nyasaland on the other. Yet production i
the two areas is widely divergent, Southern Rhodesia hav
ing an output of about 150 million pounds a year, twic
the figure for the rest of the Federation.

In the early days of Commonwealth tobacco, some at
tempts to popularize it went too far and backfired. As th

mperial Economic Committee dryly commented in its
eport on the commodity in 1937, 'Some manufacturers
pressed on the attention of the public under the general
description of Empire some mixtures etc. whose chief advertising point was their cheapness – a policy of doubtful
wisdom.'

However, it is fair to say that Commonwealth tobaccos
have now lived down their earlier dubious reputation. Be-
ween 1951 and 1961 there was an interesting change in the
composition of the tobacco retained in this country by
manufacturers. In the earlier year imports totalled 290
million pounds, of which thirty-six per cent was Commonwealth. Of this 219 million pounds was retained for home
consumption, and about forty-three per cent was Commonwealth. In contrast, by 1961 imports had advanced to 318
million pounds in total, or by nearly ten per cent. But non-
Commonwealth tobacco actually declined by ten per cent,
so that Commonwealth growths expanded by fully forty-
five per cent and accounted for forty-eight per cent of
combined imports. The change in retained imports was
even sharper: from foreign countries there was a decline
of nearly two per cent, whereas Commonwealth supplies
rose by almost fifty per cent to over 135 million pounds
and made up fifty-two per cent of the 260 million pounds
retained.

The pattern of imports is now approximately as is shown
in Table 7.

The importance of Britain as a customer for tobacco
varies widely from country to country. Table 8 shows total
output in the producing countries from which Britain buys,
together with their total exports of tobacco and the proportion of their income from foreign trade which tobacco
represents.

Britain buys just about half of Rhodesia's tobacco, and

css–5

thus accounts for ten per cent of the Federation's total income. This is the biggest impact which Britain has: although two-thirds of Canada's tobacco exports come here, this accounts for barely a quarter of one per cent of Canada's export income. Similarly, despite the fact that Britain

Table 7.

	million lb.
Rhodesia, Nysaland	75
Canada	20
India	45
	140
U.S.A.	160
Turkey	2
Greece	1
	163
	303

Table 8.

	Tobacco		Value of exports (£ m)	Percentage of exports of all goods
	Production (m. lb.)	Exports (m. lb.)		
Rhodesia, Nyasaland	200	150	28	20
Canada	200	30	6	0·4
India	530	100	17	3
U.S.A.	1,750	500	120	2
Turkey	230	190	36	34
Greece	190	140	27	36

buys nearly half of her tobacco exports, India derives only one and a half per cent of her current foreign earnings from this source. In the case of the United States, still this country's largest single supplier, Britain takes a third of the tobacco exported, but this brings in less than one per cent of the American export income.

If Britain were to cease buying tobacco from abroad, her own balance of payments would not show any sharp improvement. On the one hand just about £100 million a year would be saved on imports, but as against this our own exports of cigarettes would presumably come to a halt, and these are now bringing in around £20 million. On balance we could thus expect to save about £80 million on our visible trade accounts – about two months' average gap between imports and exports. This, though it would be welcome, would not be a striking contribution to the task of rebuilding the country's economic strength.

On the other side of the account, suspension of British tobacco purchases would have a serious adverse effect on Rhodesia, and would have to be accompanied by special measures to make good the loss – which would themselves largely offset the benefit to the payments position described above. Elsewhere there would be very little perceptible effect on the other national economies, although individual growers and traders with strong links with British buyers would obviously have to contend with difficulties of their own.

Indeed, the principal effect of any withdrawal of Britain from the ranks of smoking nations would probably show in a decline of tobacco prices: there would, after all, be a drop of thirty per cent in world trade and of about six per cent in free-world consumption, which would find reflection in a sharp drop in prices – the more so since most countries levy heavy taxes on tobacco. A substantial fall has therefore to occur in leaf prices before there is a sufficient lowering of prices at the retail level to make possible a stimulation of demand on the scale that would be required.

Even so, and apart from the special case of Rhodesia, the British contribution to the world economy arising from the country's smoking habits is not so great as to have more than local and secondary effects.

If the economic consequences of nicotine at home and abroad are not large – the main interests to be affected by ruling it out being small shopkeepers, television advertising executives, and Southern Rhodesia – it remains to consider the adverse consequences that arise from the present situation, and which must be set off against the losses already discussed in arriving at a true balance sheet.

To begin with a comparatively small example of what may be regarded as the social cost of smoking, there are the fires which smokers cause. Of course it is not necessary to ban smoking for the losses caused in this way to be avoided, but, as things are, smoking leads to many thousands of fires each year, and the damage and injuries involved can properly be regarded as a debit item.

Between 1956 and 1958 the number of fires inside buildings fluctuated very narrowly at around 51,000. But the number, and the proportion, which started from smokers' materials rose sharply: 4,440 in 1956; 4,971 in 1957; and 5,264 in 1958 – an increase of nearly twenty per cent. In 1959 there was a very steep rise in the number of fires, which jumped to 61,328. But those for which smokers were responsible went up even faster, to 6,940. In 1960 the total again increased, but only by about 1,000, whereas the rise in smokers' fires was twice as great. Hence, whereas in 1956 only one fire in twelve of those inside buildings was caused by smoking, the proportion in 1960 had gone up to more than one in nine.

A similar trend has emerged in the more numerous fires that occur outdoors. In 1956, 6,508 outbreaks out of a total of 71,704 were attributed to smokers. The total dropped for the next two years, and was followed down by smokers' fires only in 1958. 1959 was an extraordinary year: presumably reflecting the last blazing summer we enjoyed, the number of outdoor fires multiplied nearly fourfold to over 176,000. But smokers responded, too, with a more than sixfold increase to over 28,000. 1960 brought a comparative return to sanity, with the total of outbreaks back to its 1956 level of 71,000. However, smokers were responsible in 9,300 cases, or thirteen per cent, compared with only nine per cent four years earlier. There have been several complaints that woodland fires have been started by careless smokers, although no direct connexion with the idyllic advertisements showing young lovers lighting each other's cigarettes has been proved.

All in all, about one fire in eight is caused by smoking. As the annual damage done by fire runs to about £80 million, this suggests that £10 million is attributable to smokers.

Every working day in this country nearly a million people are away from work through illness. The annual loss is about 200 million days, which dwarfs the three million to eight million days lost in recent years through strikes, about which there is a great deal of indignation. Much of the condemnatory energy involved might more usefully be channelled towards a reduction of industrial losses arising from the smoking habit. In the course of a year twenty-seven million days are lost through bronchitis – an eighth of the total, and about five times the numbers lost through strikes. Granted that the British climate encourages bronchitis without any contribution from tobacco, there can be little doubt but that smoking aggravates the condition even if it plays little part in causation. If twenty per cent of the time lost in industry through bronchitis can be attributed to the effects of smoking, then this aspect of smoking alone causes as much economic damage as all the strikes that take place each year. And that this is not

an implausible proportion is suggested by the findings of
three surveys quoted in the Royal College Report showing
that over thirty per cent of smokers suffer from persistent
coughing of a bronchitic type as compared with about eight
per cent of non-smokers.

No calculation can be made of the loss attributable to
other illness that arises, or is aggravated, by smoking, but
the figure is certainly not nil. Even on the basis of five
million days lost because of bronchitis the annual amount
of lost production would be about £15 million.

Another important social cost is the large number of
disabled people, many of them rendered unfit for work by
disease, and some of them undoubtedly affected by
illness caused or aggravated by smoking. There are about
650,000 people on the disabled register, and nearly ten per
cent of them are there because of bronchitis or other conditions affecting the lungs. Again, the cost cannot be cal-
culated, but it cannot be ignored: nor can the strain on our
overloaded medical profession and hospitals of caring for
those requiring attention because of their smoking habits –
quite apart from the public money required to meet their
drug bills and to pay for the services of specialists and
other staff.

Finally we come to one of the biggest items of all: the
cost to the community of the premature deaths of many
of its members who are smokers. Without making any as-
sumptions as to the causative agents involved, it is clearly
established that a smoker has, at all ages over twenty-five, a
shorter expectation of life than a non-smoker. The differences are not substantial until after the age of thirty-five,
but they are linked quite clearly with the amount of
smoking.

Bearing in mind that male smokers, who outnumber
women smokers by about three to two, average nineteen

cigarettes a day against ten for women, the average consumption is about sixteen daily. Mortality rates for smokers and non-smokers have been worked out from a study based on British doctors, and the figures for those smoking between fifteen and twenty-four cigarettes a day may reasonably be taken as indicating the prospects for smokers in general.

The tables can be interpreted to show that for every 1,000 non-smokers who reach the age of thirty-five, eleven will die before they reach forty-four. Among smokers the corresponding figure is sixteen. There is thus an excess mortality rate of 0·5 per cent per 1,000 per annum among smokers in this age group. The differential in favour of non-smokers increases with age, and Table 9 shows the number of survivors that may be expected from 1,000 smokers and 1,000 non-smokers at various ages.

Table 9.

	Survivors		Excess mortality
	Non-smokers	Smokers	
35–44	989	984	5
45–54	952	914	33
55–64	838	729	71
65–74	574	423	42

Thus, eighty-four per cent of non-smokers aged thirty-five can expect to live to sixty-five, the normal retirement age for men, whereas only seventy-three per cent of smokers can do so.

Now, it is possible to calculate approximately the loss involved by this differential life expectation. Out of every 1,000 smokers five more will die within ten years than is the case with non-smokers. They will lose an average of twenty-five working years each. In the next age-bracket the thirty-three who die early as compared with the non-smokers lose fifteen years each, while in the fifty-five to sixty-four group seventy-one will lose about five years each on average. This make a total of 975 man-years for each thousand smokers. Applying this to a population of twenty-one million smokers, the indicated loss as they move from thirty-five to sixty-five is 20,875,000 years – almost precisely one year per smoker and an average shortening of life expectation of nine and a half years for each of the 2·2 million who must face the fact that they will die before the normal time.

If the deaths were spread evenly over the thirty-year period, which would not in fact happen in practice as the death-rate among smokers rises more than proportionately to age, there would be just over 70,000 excess deaths each year. In actual fact, since the population of smokers is already distributed among the various age-groups, the annual loss of man-years is also already reflecting deaths that occurred prematurely many years ago, as well as those that take place this year. Thus, we are currently deprived of the equivalent of nearly 700,000 man years: 70,000 deaths a year each costing nine and a half years, or, alternatively, a thirtieth of twenty-one million man-years each year.

At the average annual rate of productivity among employed people, a man-year is worth about £1,200 in gross output. Hence the annual gross loss because of the depletion of the population by the excess of mortality among smokers is running at over £800 million, or about three per cent of the national income. This is a startling figure, and indeed the first we have come across to compare with the revenue which the Government derives from tobacco.

It does not of course simply follow that the economy could save this sum each year if everybody stopped smoking. Even assuming that the excess mortality eased at once, and did not prove to have a more abstruse cause, the net gains would be much smaller. The people who would live longer would naturally consume as well as produce, and require imports as well as making exports. But with many sectors of industry chronically short of labour despite short-term fluctuations, the prospective 700,000 man-years that would become available annually would probably provide £840 million more output. Of this about a third might be exported, while, if additional imports could be kept down to £200 million, £80 million would be available to buttress the balance of payments.

At home the extra lease of life would simultaneously boost trade and result in less pressure of demand on medical services. The first would be more than proportional to the size of the 700,000 man-years to the population because a high percentage of them would be earning and spending incomes. There would probably be a rise of over £500 million in the nation's retail trade, or about three per cent, while the saving on hospital care and medical treatment can hardly be put at less than £50 million.

Aside from these changes, the State would also benefit directly. Payments for sickness benefit would be cut, as would other items of social security, while the National Health Service would presumably benefit from reduced pressure and increased flexibility to a greater extent than the mere reduction in expenditure indicates. But the most striking effect would be on the revenue. Incomes would rise by about £1,000 million a year if excess mortality among smokers were abolished overnight and no other disease immediately took away this gain. At present rates of direct and indirect taxation this would yield £300 million, so that it is by no means far-fetched to suggest that, if the elimination of tobacco had the consequences suggested, about half the loss of revenue from it would be made good automatically. On top of this the ending of our overseas trade in tobacco, and the effect of higher production, should improve our net export-import position by at least £120 million.

It is of course unrealistic to expect such changes to come about quickly even if a decision were taken to discourage or prohibit smoking tomorrow. These calculations are however of value as showing where gains and losses would accrue were the smoking habit gradually to diminish from now on through a smaller proportion of each successive generation taking it up. While hopes of an apocalyptic change are clearly ill-founded, the possible economic benefits go a long way to offset the losses – quite apart from the question of human suffering.

One surprising fact is that the life assurance offices have not taken account of the clearly established mortality differential between smokers and non-smokers in setting their premium rates. This differential is certainly actuarially significant, but no company has yet incorporated it. This is the more unexpected in that motor insurance on favourable terms is already available to abstainers from alcoholic drink, and the problem of detecting lapses among non-smokers is, if anything, easier than among non-abstaining drivers. The effect of nicotine on lung tissue is inescapable if taken in any quantity, and this would show up on post-mortem examination, whereas many of the claims made by drivers under abstainers' insurance policies occur in circumstances which do not allow of any immediate check for alcohol.

In conclusion, I would venture two observations not directly connected with the economics of the case, but which have some bearing. It seems that the bigger the vested interest the higher the standard of proof demanded. There is a great outcry and an almost immediate ban on any new substance which may have harmful effects if included in food: an ingredient used in Blackpool rock which may occasionally cause cancer in certain conditions was rapidly outlawed as soon as it came under suspicion. Tobacco is still not subject to active prosecution, although if tobacco growing were an industry confined to, say, the West Country, together with the medical statistics concerning lung cancer, who can doubt that it would have been stopped a long time ago?

My other suggestion is for a happy ending that might satisfy almost all the participants in the cigarette-lung-cancer imbroglio. The suggestion may prove well-founded that the American lung-cancer rate is lower than the British, despite higher consumption, because smokers in the United States leave longer stubs. If so, then the manufacturers could sell twice as many cigarettes; the Government could cut the rate of tax by half without losing revenue; both parties could spend a lot of money advertising that everybody should throw the second half of every cigarette away, and tobacco addicts could smoke as much as they liked without fear. Perhaps this should, however, be aptly dismissed as a pipe-dream.

THE SOCIAL IMPLICATIONS

Lena Jeger

CIGARETTES have not always stuck out of mouths any
more than rings have everywhere been put through noses.
The acceptability of the human face with a manufactured
proboscis attached to it is a comparatively recent phenome-
non. This fact has to be stressed because the most im-
penetrable thought-barrier surrounding the smoking habit
is the idea that smoking is as natural a function as eating
or drinking, and that those who think otherwise are the
eccentrics, the deviationists. 'Non-smoker' has acquired a
slightly pejorative inflexion in recent times, a hint of the
crank, the faddist, the neurotic, close to the vegetarian, the
pacifist, fresh-air fiend, noise abater, and members of other
minority pressure groups. Unless the web of thought about
the social naturalness of smoking can be broken through,
no isolated campaign, whether based on fear or on fervour,
can succeed.

In fact the history of the smoking habit in this country
is as varied as a hectic temperature chart. Before considering all the modern pressures that suggest the indispensabil-
ity of the cigarette to romance, relaxation, concentration,
verility, femininity, sophistication, it is essential to peel off
some layers of social history, of anthropology and colonial
economics. Between the over-simplification of those who
explain away smoking habits as merely nipple-sucking sub-
stitutes and the complications of modern advertising techniques there is a long and highly relevant story.

The pipe has of course an old and ritual significance in

many societies. The symbol of smoking the pipe of peace, for instance, which signified that it was safe for erstwhile enemies to come close together, is deeply established in the human psyche. In fact human beings are the only animals who deliberately take smoke into their bodies. They have done this for centuries through the burning of incense in their holy places, through the pleasure of pulling through paper tubes, twists of leaves, pipes of wood or clay, to get the touch of smoke into themselves. The inhalation of smoke is older than the introduction of tobacco to Europe. Reeds, pipes, and tubes of all sorts are to be found in many Greco-Roman remains and the great Hippocrates prescribed smoke inhalation for asthma and certain other ailments, but the smoke came from dried cow dung, or herbs such as coltsfoot. In the Middle Ages in this country the smoking of herbs was sometimes advised for 'windy griefs of the breast'. There are still people who compromise by smoking 'herbal mixtures', to give themselves the comfort of sucking without the dangers of nicotine.

This is not the place for an exhaustive study of the antiquity of the habit of smoking in its various forms. The current controversy concerns the smoking of tobacco, especially in the form of cigarettes. Suffice it to say that tobacco as we know it was presented to the first European, Columbus, in 1492 in the Bahamas.

I found [Columbus wrote] a man alone in a canoe who was going from the island of Santa Maria to Fernandina. He had some dry leaves which must be a thing very much appreciated among them, because they had already brought me some as a present at San Salvador.

Here is the implant of a persistent etiquette, the predecessor of the modern manifestation of the conventional good manners of welcome. Some of the explorers whom Columbus sent ashore with Spanish guides reported seeing

natives who 'drank smoke'. In his journal Columbus wrote
of 'many people who always carry a lighted firebrand to
light fire and to perfume themselves with certain herbs'.

The chewing of what must have been tobacco was also
remarked by the early explorers of the new world. In 1499
Amerigo Vespucci noticed off the coast of Venezuela that
the natives 'all had their cheeks swollen out with a green
herb inside, which they were constantly chewing like beasts
so that they could scarcely utter speech'. Clearly they were
the forebears of the intolerable men of today who expect
one to understand what they say as they mutter out of one
side of their mouths, their teeth clenched on a pipe which
renders them incoherent. (One should never try to make out
what men say if they talk with pipes in their mouths. If
you say 'I beg your pardon?' often enough, most men
eventually take out their spitty pipes to repeat their words
in high tolerant voices to the apparently deaf.)

As a matter of interest Vespucci noticed that the women
did not chew tobacco. At the same time an industrious friar,
Ramon Pané, whom Columbus had sent to Haiti to investigate conditions, reported on the inhalation of what must
have been snuff. Meanwhile the word 'tobacco' was born
with the report of Indians who inhaled smoke through a
Y-shaped pipe, inserting the two forks of the Y into their
nostrils. They called this pipe a 'tabaco'.

It seemed that the early discoverers regarded tobacco as
stuff for native savages and at the beginning of the sixteenth
century there was little in the writings of the explorers to
suggest that this primitive habit was to become centuries
later the symbol of Western sophistication. If it had only
been the 'tabaco' pipe that had been met, the influence on
Western Europe might have been minimal. But Spaniards
in Cuba also came across the primitive form of the
cigar.

The hedonistic novelty of what must have been a very crude pleasure quickly asserted itself and became economically of even greater significance than all the gold and silver that future slaves were to dig for the white man out of the mines. Socially in Europe smoking became associated with tough men, because it was explorers who brought tobacco to Europe and explorers were usually the brave and reckless, the pace-setters of the golden ages of discovery.

As far as one can tell, the tobacco plant ironically was first brought to Europe by a physician, Francisco Hernandes, who had been sent to Mexico on a voyage of exploration by Philip II of Spain. The French ambassador to Portugal, Jean Nicot, sent seeds of the plant to the Queen Mother of France, Catherine de' Medici, and it is after him that the scientific name 'nicotiana' and its derivatives (such as 'nicotine') are used. Although some knowledge of tobacco came to England through Spain, there is evidence that Ralph Lane, the first governor of Virginia, was a smoker, and in 1586 Francis Drake brought tobacco to England, sending some to Sir Walter Raleigh. Earlier – probably about 1565, Sir John Hawkins had brought some seeds from Florida, but it was Raleigh who promoted the use of the plant for smoking. At this time tobacco was smoked through pipes and this quickly became a habit at the court of Elizabeth, some historians maintaining that the good queen herself was not averse to puffing at a pipe. Certainly Sir Walter Raleigh was allowed the comfort of a pipe of tobacco just before he went to the scaffold in 1618 on Tower Hill.

At the end of the sixteenth and through the seventeenth centuries the habit of smoking spread like a fire throughout Europe. The sanatory powers of the tobacco herb were hailed at a time when there was something of a standstill in European medicine and novelties were welcome. Much en-

couragement was given by Nicot himself, who asserted that
the 'Indian herb' had marvellous curative powers and that
it had dealt with ulcers and eliminated a fistula. Tobacco
in its various forms became the placebo of European
medicine. This is part of the irony of history – that it was
the doctors (and some churchmen) of seventeenth-century
Europe who were the main propagandists for the use of the
weed that many now want to deplore. During the Great
Plague in England ('1664–6) the boys at Eton were made
to smoke a pipe of tobacco each day for the good of their
health. When Pepys saw the cross of death on the plague
doors he wrote that he was 'forced to buy some roll tobacco
to smell and to chaw, which took away the apprehension'.
Tobacco was an accepted item in the pharmacopeia. Smoke
enemas were used for various internal complaints – a sort
of bellows forcing smoke up the rectum. The medicinal use
of tobacco in fact preceded the social habit of smoking and
many tracts warned against the indiscriminate use of
tobacco otherwise than when prescribed by physicians.
Meanwhile in other parts of the travelled world, in the
Middle East, Africa, distant China, the smoking habit was
spreading fast in many forms other than medicinal.

Fashion, for all its wayward inconsistencies, has been a
vital factor in deciding the consumption of tobacco. For the
dandies in the early seventeenth century it was essential – a
selection of fair and expensive pipes was part of a gentleman's equipment. The fads of the well-to-do have always
been the ambition of the social climber and Jonson referred
to this necessary habit:

It may seem strange to enumerate taking tobacco among the
accomplishments to be acquired in town, but it was then a
matter of serious study and had its professors, like the rest of
the liberal arts.

Probably it was the excessive use of tobacco and its association with the idle fops of the day which helped to inspire the first serious anti-smoking campaign, led by James I with his *Counterblaste to Tobacco*, published in 1604. The King may have been prejudiced against tobacco because its use in this country was associated with Raleigh, whom he hated unto death. And the dour Scot in him was outraged by all the effete sybaritic tendencies of the young English gallants, of which their smoking was but one. James I however also seems to have taken prophetic notice of the warnings of some doctors, for he wrote, in what might have been a Stuart preface to the report published in 1962 by the Royal College of Physicians, that because of 'the precious stink' autopsies revealed that the inward parts of heavy smokers were 'soiled and infected with an oily kind of soot'. He also tried to shame people from smoking by pointing out that the Indians used tobacco as a specific against venereal disease and that English gentlemen who smoked were risking the insinuation that they needed tobacco to cure them of the shameful sickness. At the same time James and his supporters threatened smokers with other afflictions of their virility.

> Tobacco, that outlandish weed,
> It spends the brain and spoils the seed.
> It dulls the sprite, it dims the sight,
> It robs a woman of her right.

But opposition to smoking in England never reached the perilous sanctions imposed in Russia in 1634, when the use of tobacco was prohibited. First offenders – buyers, sellers, or smokers – had their noses slit and were whipped. Sentence of death could be passed on persistent offenders, or deportation to Siberia.

During the seventeenth century laws were passed prohibiting smoking in Denmark, Sweden, the Netherlands,

Sicily, Austria, and Hungary. But these restrictions do not seem to have been any more effective than no-smoking rules at modern schools. Smoking was so common, especially in Spain, that Pope Urban VIII had to issue a bull threatening excommunication to those who smoked or took snuff in church. Later popes tried to renew the edict.

All this is more relevant to our present dilemma than may be apparent. For it must be understood that the habit of smoking has proved invincible before the majesty of tsar, pope, and king. Men risked their souls and their bodies to persist in their slavery to nicotine. So the law by itself can be of little avail where there is no willing public consent or understanding of its purpose. It is therefore not to the making of rules alone that one can look for a reduction in smoking, although public discipline has its part to play.

Nor have attempts to control smoking by taxation been successful. When James I first levied heavy taxes on tobacco he intended the taxes to act as a disincentive, an indication of his moral disapproval, rather than as revenue raisers. But the latter function quickly predominated. Meanwhile in Virginia tobacco was fast becoming the essential product vital to colonial economics. The whole tobacco traffic became a vast vested interest. Charles I, who also disliked smoking, added to his revenues by taxing tobacco shops as well as tobacco imports. Attempts to grow tobacco in England were made illegal in order to protect the colonial growers, but England became increasingly the European trading centre for tobacco.

Gradually the legal strictures against smoking collapsed everywhere before its golden economics. Switzerland persisted longer than anywhere, especially in Berne, where the council bracketed smoking with adultery and until about the middle of the eighteenth century the penalties were the same: prison, pillory, and fine. But in Russia, for example,

Peter the Great (1672–1725) abolished all restrictions and smoking was accepted as part of westernization.

Society looks all the time for novelty. After this country had settled down comfortably to its smoking habits there came in the early eighteenth century the new practice of 'snuffing'. Snuff, which is basically powdered tobacco, was sniffed up the nose, immediately provoking a succession of sneezes which were found to be refreshing, and no doubt the odour of the snuff was a pleasant antidote to the habitual bad smells of the time. Large quantities of snuff were first brought to England in 1702 when Spanish ships loaded with it were seized at Vigo Bay. There was of course an earlier history to the sniffing of herbs, but it was the eighteenth century which was the glorious age of snuff. It became as universal as the chewing of gum in the United States today. These waves of habit, which come and go, may be the best hope of the anti-smokers. Nothing is fixed in human affairs, least of all in the social habits of human pleasure. The sniffing, sneezing, snorting, hawking, and eructations which were part of the process of snuffing became acceptable good manners in the highest society of the eighteenth century, especially in England and France. Here in the eighteenth century there were over a hundred different kinds of snuff: coloured with ochres, perfumed with musk, bergamot, cloves, cedar, and other substances. Elegant labels and wrappers with the different names on were the genesis of modern advertising. The making of snuff boxes became one of the highest forms of craftsmanship.

Smoking seemed to decrease as snuffing took over. Dr Johnson wrote in 1773 in *The Journal of a Tour to the Hebrides*:

Smoaking has gone out. To be sure, it is a shocking thing, blowing smoak out of our mouths into other people's mouths, eyes, and noses and having the same thing done to us. Yet I cannot account why a thing which requires so little exertion, and yet preserves the mind from total vacuity, should have gone out.

In the view of Professor G. M. Trevelyan, smoking stayed 'out' for about eighty years – not that there was no smoking, but that it was not, in modern idiom 'with it' to smoke. It is the indefinable assertion of fashion again which affected the change. It may well be that the time has come here and now for such a change of habit, and that the pen-dulum will swing with only slight assistance from the warnings of doctors. But it must be remembered that in the eighteenth century smoking went out partly because snuff-ing was in.

The decrease in smoking among the upper classes was also in part due to a general improvement in manners.

Nobody could accuse Beau Nash (1674–1762), one of England's most famous dandies, of lacking in the arts of pleasure and self-indulgence. He was master of ceremonies at Bath in its great days of high fashion – in fact his efforts largely made it so. But Nash firmly forbade smoking in the public rooms at Bath as being disrespectful and unpleasant for the ladies. Perhaps this rule was the more acceptable because it was part of an attempt by Nash – largely suc-cessful – to bring a little more grace into life. Along with restrictions on smoking he stopped the habit of gentlemen wearing swords in places of amusement, frowned on duel-ling, encouraged the wearing by gentlemen of stockings and shoes, rather than boots. From this time the bigger country houses tended to have their 'smoking parlour' and guests would not be expected to smoke elsewhere.

Gradually the assertion of the intangible 'not-done' criterion of good manners caused the smoking of tobacco to be regarded as 'low' or 'fast', fit only for soldiers and the vulgar people. Snuffing too tended to fade as a habit, first in France after the Revolution because it was indelibly associated with the aristocracy.

After the Peninsular War (1809–14), when Britain defeated the French in Spain, the army discovered the cigar in a big way – previously little used in England. Cigar smoking became increasingly fashionable – even ladies smoked little cigars called 'queens'. But there was one brake on the smoking habit in the last century. Queen Victoria came to the throne in 1837. Her Majesty could not abide smoking, and this inevitably set some pattern of mores.

But once more war changed the course of smoking habits. A little roll of tobacco, called a cigarette, had been gaining popularity on the Continent and in America. Something like the cigarette had been known in Mexico, India, and Siam for a long time, but the modern cigarette became usual in Europe only in the nineteenth century. When the British went off to fight the Crimean War (1854–6) they found their French and especially their Turkish allies smoking cigarettes, sometimes rolled by themselves. Pipes got broken in war; cigars were dear and distant. The little cigarette was the answer and the British soldiers brought home this new fashion which was to give a tremendous momentum to smoking habits in this country and to start a vogue which has been steadily growing ever since, a fashion which has become a vast industry. This increase in smoking occurred despite the displeasure of the famous commander, the Duke of Wellington, who shared Queen Victoria's opposition to smoking. In 1854 he issued a general order asking regimental commanders to stop the practice of smoking in mess-rooms and to dissuade junior officers from continuing the habit. But in this campaign the gallant Duke was doomed to defeat. Cigarettes were at first imported, but about 1856 a Greek named Theodori started a cigarette factory here. The production of cigarettes was for a long time in the hands of foreign settlers, especially Polish and Russian Jews who had fled to England to escape persecution.

Nevertheless Queen Victoria continued her veto, useless as Mrs Partington's mop to stop the growing habit, but at least causing some limitations of seemliness to be imposed. Modern parents, anxious about their children smoking, can learn little from Queen Victoria's rigorous no-smoking rules. For Edward VII was a regular smoker, even though, before his mother's death, he had to go away from the Palace to smoke. The Marlborough Club, for example, was established about 1868 by the Prince of Wales and a group of friends for the purpose of 'securing a convenient and agreeable place of meeting for a society of gentlemen'. The establishment of this club was part of the protest of the Prince not only against his mother's ferocious anti-smoking rules, but against the restrictions imposed on smoking at some other clubs, especially White's. Most clubs of repute had their smoking-rooms, so that at least the whole place did not reek of tobacco.

It is thought that from the Prince of Wales there originated the traditional toast-master's announcement at the proper point of formal functions. It seems that at the first royal banquet after his accession, the new King looked kindly at all the deprived, long-suffering gentlemen gathered in the coffee-room. There had been no smoking in this place for over sixty years. In a few words came a Palace revolution. 'Gentlemen', said His Majesty, 'you may smoke.'

The Victorians were more careful about the smell of tobacco – perhaps so as not to offend their ladies who sometimes liked to emulate the delicacy of the Queen in these matters. Smoking-jackets were worn so that clothes should not smell, even smoking-caps to protect the hair from noxious odours. 'Having a smoke' was an activity on its own, not a casual accompaniment of work or play.

Although by the latter part of the nineteenth century smoking was increasing, we had still not reached the point of today's acceptability of smoking almost anywhere and at almost any time. There were for instance, cigar divans in London to which gentlemen wishing for a smoke took themselves. Trollope describes in *The Warden* (1882) how Mr Harding, with time on his hands in London, visited a cigar shop with a divan above it, which he found 'very civil'.

Of course anti-smoking societies were active all this time, both here and in America. But the increasing cigarette industry was busily expanding with all the devices of a developing sales-promotion campaign, including the advent of the cigarette card. All, however was not lost from Queen Victoria's point of view. At least ladies, unless very daring, did not smoke in public. Even in France, when *Carmen* (sub-titled 'The Cigarette Maker's Romance') was first performed in 1876 the co-director of the Opéra Comique, de Leuven, was said to be as horrified at the smoking chorus in the first act as at the final murder, as both might spoil the performance for family outings. As late as 1909, Wolf-Ferrari's opera *Il Segreto di Susanna* depended for its plot on the discovery of a wife's guilty secret – this turned out to be not that she had a lover, but that she was guilty of smoking secretly. This was accepted as a valid enough plot – an indication of an outlook different from today's.

In this country smoking on the stage was to become increasingly familiar – sometimes as part of the dialogue or stage directions, sometimes merely to give the actor something to do with his hands. Shaw was always very clear about this – if he wanted his characters to smoke he said so, as for example in Act 1 of *Widowers' Houses* (1892) he describes Trench as striking a match and proceeding to light his pipe. In *Mrs Warren's Profession* (1894), Vivie says:

> ... Pass the cigar box, will you?
> FRANK: Nasty womanly habit. Nice men don't do it any more.
> VIVIE: Yes. They object to the smell in the office and we've had
> to take to cigarettes. See! [*She opens the box and takes out*
> *a cigarette which she lights.*]

This is an interesting contrast to modern attempts to urge a switch the other way round – away from cigarettes to cigars, as less harmful.

But again in this century it was war that caused another gigantic increase in smoking. 'As long as you've a Lucifer to light your fag . . .' became as well known as the first line of the National Anthem. This generation can never know what trench warfare of the First World War was like – most of them do not even bother to read Wilfred Owen, to open their minds to *Journey's End, All Quiet on the Western Front, Death of a Hero.* Many old men of today started smoking in the mud and cold and blood of the flooded ditches of danger which were the habitat of their ravaged youth in the First World War. Some hoped it would frighten the rats to see a glow; some thought it kept the lice away. Many will tell you that a fag helped to pass the time of endless waiting. But mostly there was no rationalization. Why should there be? Sending 'smokes' to the troops became one of the few things that a guilty, helpless civilian society could do. Certainly there was never any reason in either of the great wars of this century to doubt that em-battled men and women wanted cigarettes. Nowadays, many of the young people who are starting to smoke have never known or needed the desperate, passing comfort of smoking under intolerable strain; but this was how many of their grandfathers and fathers began – began and never stopped. So it became part of the household life; the ashtray took its place as an indispensable article of furniture and decoration. Often mothers smoke too. What is there left to say to the present generation?

The modern problem primarily concerns the children. The others of us can dree our own weird. What we did at first in ignorance and later in the chains of habit has been overtaken by knowledge which we did not have, but which we dare not fail to use for the young generation. Those most in contact with children obviously have to make an effort not to smoke, or at least to explain smoking to their children almost as an affliction, an aberration. Children today are subjected to an environment which suggests that smoking is natural, taken for granted, and that it is the non-smoker who is deprived and aberrant.

Clearly parents who smoke are at a disadvantage in trying to restrain their children. But nothing is lost if the smoking habits of older people can be linked to some specific period of strain or difficulty which can be explained to the children, instead of leaving them to think that smoking is as inevitable as eating, drinking, and loving. It is not easy to convince children about the advantages of not smoking if they are used to seeing their parents with cigarettes, watch them offer cigarettes as a ritual to callers, give cigarettes or other adjuncts of smoking for festive presents, see the relaxation of the evening grow around the pipe, the slippers by the fire; experience the trauma of irritation when an adult gives up smoking. At the same time the parent may be beloved, adored, an example in all things. How, in this one matter, can the feet of clay be suggested without disloyalty?

It is something if parents regretfully explain their addiction – this is more use than downright prohibition, a negative attitude of 'do as I say, not as I do'. Without seeming mean it is also possible to contract one's hospitality by not having full boxes of cigarettes lying around for automatic offer. If you make children think it is part of the good manners of adult society to be always pushing cigarettes at visitors they unconsciously absorb the useless etiquette of nicotine distribution.

The teacher who feels guilty about his surreptitious pipe may well conclude that any sacrifice is wasted on his part as his pupils see every day newspapers and hoardings and television commercials full of the praise of various tobaccos or cigarettes. Even more insidious, in advertisements for other goods – e.g. for beer or handmade shoes, or suntan oil – the envied prototype man or woman is often depicted smoking. In newspaper photographs of famous personalities, or ordinary people suddenly in the news, the pipe or cigarette is often an automatic part of the picture. To suggest affluence the cigar appears.

Of course it is not only smoking which receives this over-emphasis. But two things are special about smoking in our advertisement-sodden community – first that the investment in smoking in all its forms and including all its paraphernalia is high in a society short of productive capital investment; secondly that it is now clinically certain that tobacco is definitely harmful, and its advertisement should logically be as unacceptable to a sane society as would be advertisements for any other form of self-damage drug addiction, for example.

Instead, famous people lend their names to exploitation by tobacco firms. Every effort is made by a clever and resourceful advertising industry to suggest that smoking has to do with romance, with confidence and success, with relaxation or with concentration, whichever suits. The build-up persists of the successful man or woman not properly dressed without a cigarette or a pipe in their mouths. The completely gullible might well accept the cigarette as an extra feature of the face.

Advertising is dealt with in detail elsewhere in this book. Suffice it to say here that any restriction or limitation on advertising is bound to make some difference, however small, in reducing the environmental encouragement to smoke, and must be welcomed. The Italian Government has passed legislation (Law No. 65, effective from 29 April 1962) forbidding any form of advertisement for tobacco and sundry products connected with smoking – either produced in Italy or imported. It will be interesting to see the effect of this on consumption – and on revenue. Tobacco is, in any case, a government monopoly in Italy. But the reduction of any government's income from tobacco duty must be offset against the incalculable cost of smoking. One would hope that any responsible government, weighing these problems, would not look only for an arithmetical answer. But if they did, they would need to include the cost to the National Health Service, and to individuals, of illness attributable to or aggravated by smoking, of time lost from work, the immense part of the public cleaning bills spent on clearing the litter of smoking from passenger vehicles, railway stations, streets, and offices, etc. And the proportion of the total cost of fire destruction and damage to be charged against the national smoking account runs into several million pounds.

It has been seen from the brief historical facts previously mentioned that the whole answer to this problem is not to be found in sanctions, especially as far as the addict is concerned. Measures such as the Italians are trying are of value mainly in the negative but important sense that those who do not yet smoke may continue to abstain if only for a little while longer without being made to feel that they are either freakish or missing out on some irresistible atavistic pleasure.

On the other hand, if a fraction of the costs of tobacco advertisements in this country could be used for a campaign against smoking, provided it was imaginatively conceived and sustained for many years, it could do nothing but good. Especially if as many well-known people – particularly people who are admired by boys and girls – were associated with it. Of course efforts are being made in this direction, but so far the scale is pathetically small.

The Central Council for Health Education has a special schools' project for which mobile units are available, complete with speakers, films, film strips, and literature. Leaflets and posters are available from the Chest and Heart Association, the Ministry of Health, and other organizations. Some local authorities, for instance the L.C.C., have their own leaflets for distribution to school-leavers (though surely many will have got the habit early in their school lives?). It is too early yet to assess the effects on young people. The response so far seems to indicate how difficult the problem is and what highly skilled and experienced advice is needed.

I have heard it half-seriously suggested that the most effective appeal to children would be to make them think smoking was good for them – the schoolboys of the mid seventeenth century were often sent to school with filled pipes, which they had to light when told, and take a lesson in smoking, as if this were a normal school subject, whether they liked it or not.

This point has been well taken in one of the leaflets of the Chest and Heart Association:

Now that you are nearly grown up you will have to make up your mind about smoking. Moral considerations will not help.

Puffing smoke in and out of your mouth cannot exactly be called sinful. If, as an adult, you decide to smoke you won't have the pleasure of feeling that it's forbidden. There's nothing wrong with smoking – except that you will pay for it later on.

Strict school rules against smoking may increase the surreptitious pleasures, and the possibility of punishment can increase the exhilaration. On the other hand the net consumption of cigarettes is bound to be less if smoking is not overt. It is also an obvious part of school discipline, however it may sometimes be undermined by staff and parents. But there is a tight-rope of emphasis here. I have been in schools where there were so many posters, so many 'chinwags' against smoking that the whole subject assumed vast proportions. 'I'm sure,' one boy said 'that I wouldn't think half so much about smoking if they didn't keep on about it all the time.' He smoked, with his parent's consent, three or four a day. Neither he nor his friends would accept any arguments about smoking being bad while in training – they insisted that all their best 'chaps' had a few cigarettes and that those who didn't weren't any better footballers, swimmers, or cricketers.

One of the problems, especially for adolescents trying not to smoke, is the very real need which many feel urgently for something to do with their hands, for some little social grace of contact, the ice-breaking which comes with the offer of a cigarette. The pause in conversation can be covered by the striking of a match, the stubbing out of a cigarette end, the filling or knocking-out of a pipe. If people have nothing to say to each other, silence seems less awkward if they are smoking. Friendliness is suggested by the closeness of two heads bent over a light. Social confidence makes these things matter less, but they cannot be underestimated. It is important for young people to realize that for most of them smoking is in fact only a social prop; that far from being any indication of adult status or sophistication it only shows how immature, incomplete, and uncertain they are. It is part of social shyness and can be abandoned as confidence increases.

As far as girls are concerned, there have of course been times when it was considered a gesture of 'progressive' defiance, a touch of bohemian daring. The pity for girls is, however, that smoking is about the most stale and unattractive way of asserting that one is uninhibited, emancipated, or even fast. Smoking was always a pretty poor symbol of modernity, for Indian squaws have smoked through the centuries and in this country Elizabethan ladies tried it more than three and a half centuries ago.

Too much concentration on the danger of cancer does not seem to have been of maximum effect. To many children cancer is of course a terrible word; it signifies a disaster that perhaps happened to their grandfather, that may strike them in the years to come. Somehow, because it is a word of absolute calamity, it is not very acceptable within the context of their daily lives. This is in some ways ironical, because one expects the dramatic to make the maximum impression on young people. But I have found that it is no more effective, at the time, than telling them they will be killed if they go fast on motor-bikes. I say 'at the time', because nobody can ever assess what long-term effects propaganda has on people. And for every schoolboy who knows someone who died of cancer, there are hundreds to say that none of the smokers they know has died of this disease.

In some ways it is easier for them to grasp what are looked on as the lesser hazards – and this goes for grown-ups too. The tiresome chronic nuisance of coughs, bronchitis, catarrh, perhaps because they are more familiar in their own families, are often better understood. It may be that there is an emotional block about the fact that an unnecessary number of people kill themselves with cancer. 'You've got to die of SOMETHING' a pretty sixth-form girl told me. 'Why not that?' She was much more concerned about the possibility of going through life wheezing and coughing, though much too happy and healthy to be really bothered.

Dr F. M. Martin, Senior Lecturer in the Department of Public Health and Social Medicine, Edinburgh University, described in a paper at the Royal Society of Health's conference, April 1962, the failure of an anti-smoking campaign in Edinburgh. At the end of the campaign there was an increase in the number of people ready to blame smoking for coughs, catarrh, breathlessness, and bronchitis although the campaign publicity had *not* mentioned any of these ailments. There was no significant increase in the proportion mentioning cancer as a hazard of smoking, though this had been the talking-point of the campaign. Although this was not a campaign especially among children, the results are relevant.*

There is here a real challenge to the propagandists. There have been people at least since James I telling other people that smoking was bad for them. Now there is weighty clinical evidence which suggests that this is true. But the fact that something is true does not make it acceptable as a guide to human behaviour. Knowing that something is bad for us has never automatically led to its rejection.

I am only trying to suggest that, even if we were able to persuade every boy and girl of the connexion between smoking and lung cancer so that mentally they accepted it as a fact, along with the other facts of schooling, we might not be much nearer influencing their habits. We cannot base our case on a neurotic approach alone. Knowing about the

*A full report of the campaign is in the *Lancet*, 6 February 1960.

health hazard is one step. But this of itself does not eliminate the social pressures, or for some, the psychological
pressures. It does not get the smoke out of their environment.

What other appeal is there? Money is one of the most
effective. The Central Council for Health Education has one
attractive leaflet entirely on this theme. It looks rather like
a holiday brochure, advertising two weeks sun on the
Riviera, or two weeks ski holiday in the Alps, or a sight-
seeing Continental tour, all costing less than £70. On the
back it says, '20 cigarettes a day cost £70 a year and cost
much more in terms of ill-health. Which would you prefer?'
Of course it is very difficult for teachers to stress this waste
of money if parents give their children so much pocket
money that economy is not important. Comparatively high
teen-age wages make the argument less effective except when
young people are saving up for something special, or have
some absorbing interest, like buying long-playing records.

Health and money. Neither separately nor together will
these two considerations turn us into a nation of non-
smokers. They can, for children and grown-ups, be only
part of the argument. And in any case, we are not merely
conducting an argument. We are trying to interfere with a
human habit which has gone on for a very long time – in
this country for over three and a half centuries. What then
are the wider considerations which have to be discussed if
one really wants to transform the attitude of society to a
long-accepted habit? Always, of course, setting aside the
question of hopeless addiction, which needs specialist
help.

First one should begin with an apparent contradiction.
Three and a half centuries is not a very long time. Cigarettes
have been widely-smoked here for only a little over a hundred years. In that time life has radically changed in

thousands of ways. There is no essential continuity, no inevitability of something going on because it started a hundred years ago. Otherwise women and children would still be working in the pits and little boys would still be chimney sweeps, we would have operations without anaesthetics and hang people for stealing. Through the centuries we have sloughed off so many of our less agreeable habits that it is extraordinary that smoking has persisted. But it is no more impossible for people to decide to stop drawing smoke into their bodies than it was for them, at other times, to stop burning people who went to the wrong churches. The manners of people are changing all the time – think, for instance, of the use of knives and forks, of the perceptible decrease in spitting in public places, the forbidding of cock-fighting, of the elimination of much that was crude and objectionable. And of the near-finish of snuffing. Therefore, the first thing to establish, as we started this part of the book by saying, must be a flexibility of approach, an acceptance of the idea that men and women were not born with cigarettes in their mouth and that there is no reason to accept a fixation of habit as eternal and immutable.

Once one accepts the vulnerability of smoking, like other habits, to the erosion of time, fashion, and argument, there is some point in discussing the facts of the case to demonstrate, not why people should stop smoking, but why they should not start to smoke at all.

The aim must be to establish non-smoking as the norm of behaviour, rather than the exception. This can be done in many ways. From 1868, for example, railways in this country were required to provide special carriages for smokers. Gradually the emphasis has changed so that it is usually the non-smoker who is treated as the special minority on the railways today, and he who must seek for one of

the few non-smoking carriages. This situation could easily
be reversed again.

London is the most smoke-easy city I know. In Moscow,
New York, Toronto, Paris, and Stockholm for instance,
no smoking at all is allowed on the Underground. This is
accepted as normal and makes a tremendous difference, not
only to the atmosphere, but to the amount of litter which
has to be collected. I think this change in London should
be made urgently.

An increasing number of shops are asking customers not
to smoke, but in New York, for example, this is a rule in
most of the big stores – for fire prevention as well as health
reasons. Of course shops are afraid of losing business if they
impose restrictions which their competitors ignore, but it
might be worth considering whether this could not be
dealt with through by-laws, for instance, which could start
by banning smoking in food shops. This is done in Sweden.

Nowadays several theatres here ask people not to smoke
and there is no evidence of their suffering any lack of
patronage because of this. In Sweden, Finland, France, the
Soviet Union, and in parts of North America smoking is
absolutely prohibited in both cinemas and theatres. In Italy
it is forbidden in theatres but allowed in cinemas. A sensible
arrangement exists in some Canadian cinemas, in Toronto
for example, where smoking is allowed only in a special
gallery. The seats cost more and the spiralling smoke is an
interference to a minimum of other people.

Restrictions on smoking in buses and other forms of
public transport are much more severe in most other countries than here. There is, of course, no logic in our restrictions, such as they are. We do not expect people to smoke
in church – although we have shown that in the seventeenth
century they did. Nor would we expect policemen to smoke
on duty. Members of Parliament are not allowed to smoke

in the chamber or in the immediate approaches – although there is still a snuff box, permanently supplied, at the entrance to the Commons chamber. There is of course a smoking-room, which is a much less anti-social way of providing for those who must smoke than by making it generally permitted. There must be many public institutions and private undertakings where there would be no great difficulty in extending this idea. At first a vast increase in 'no-smoking' notices might be resented, and therefore resisted, unless at the same time it was possible for the confirmed smoker to go somewhere else for an occasional smoke. The point is that people should have to take some trouble if they really have to smoke.

Restriction of smoking in places where people congregate for either work or pleasure is important. The discomfort of the non-smoker in a smoke-blue office or railway carriage can be severe. But perhaps even more important is the fact that general tolerance of smoking undermines all the attempts to persuade the young not to smoke. The young are very logical. It is not always easy for them to see the justification for their own self-denial if they are forced to breathe in other people's smoke. The young secretary, for instance, with plenty of pressures urging her to smoke, can easily feel that her health is as likely to be undermined by the employer who blows smoke into her face while he dictates the letters. Of course there are scientific explanations of why smoking oneself is more harmful than being with other people who smoke, but these are often less acceptable than the rationalization of the tempted that they might as well get sick on their own smoke and enjoy it, as die without pleasure from other people's.

Just as it is difficult for people to separate in their minds their own inhaled smoke from other people's, so it is difficult for them to accept the isolated danger of tobacco smoke when they are repeatedly being told about the increasing dirtiness of the air they breathe. If tobacco smoke were the only dirt in the air, and if, by stopping smoking, people could feel they would make some sudden contribution towards a miracle of clean air, the propagandists would have an easier job.

But the contrary is true. There is evidence from the cleaner atmosphere of Australia, for instance, that there is much less lung cancer and other connected troubles among heavy smokers than there is in this country. Of course it can be argued, though not very persuasively, that because our atmosphere is so polluted already there is all the more reason why the individual should not add his personal puff of smoke. I think it would be much more effective for authority to show that it takes this question of air pollution more seriously. It is no use nagging children about the danger of smoke while the provisions of the Clean Air Act (1956) remain permissive and half-heartedly applied. After five years only 294 local authorities had published programmes and of these only 227 had confirmed orders about smoke-free zones in operation. The Beaver Committee, which reported in 1954, made clear after the disastrous smog of December 1952, that an atmosphere over London almost solid with dirt had killed a number of citizens. Of course many of the victims were old and had weak chests (perhaps made feebler through years of smoking) but in the public mind the dirt was the killer and the dirt came from chimneys and power stations. But at the 1962 conference of the Association of Public Health Inspectors it was estimated that only about 8 per cent of the total national work towards clean air had been carried out – this after eight years.

If the Government, and responsible society, wants to create a general climate of thought in which smoking is regarded as a dirty, useless, unhealthy habit, then it must tackle all sources of smoke, all causes of air pollution. And by much more stringent methods than the easy-going legislation now taking its slow and voluntary effect. There needs also to be a speed-up in the electrification of our railways. It is hard to persuade a teenager who lives in, say, Kentish Town, backing on to the railway lines where the engines 'get up steam', that his little quota of cigarette smoke is disastrous. The air is so loaded with dirt near many of our railways that the impurities are visible – usually called 'smuts' – and if authority seems tolerant or slow in dealing with the serious pollution which these people have to live with, it is rather lame to suggest that they are choking themselves with their own cigarette smoke.

It is for reasons like these that no efforts to reduce smoking can be successful as an isolated campaign. Any campaign needs to be part of a general assault on air pollution from all sources so that public opinion can become generally used to the idea that dirty air is as bad as dirty water, and that clean air is as essential as clean milk. Otherwise, especially to the young, exhortations against smoking will continue to appear slightly cranky, puritanical, and prejudiced.

Another unhelpful fact arises from the failure so far of scientists to isolate exactly what is the dangerous element in smoking. So long as nobody knows precisely which is the harmful ingredient, some cynicism persists as to whether the scientists really know what they are talking about. Now this may be most unfair, but the young *are* unfair and the dedicated smokers are resistant. This uncertainty about the precise mechanism and indentification of the deleterious substance also makes people vulnerable to claims of different methods of reducing the danger – by filter tips, for instance. Further work on the isolation and identification of the trouble-maker is bound to help the serious presentation of the case against smoking.

But this again will only be contributory. It is not in our nature to forgo things merely because they are bad for us. Pleasure has always been close to folly.

The sheer nuisance of the unaesthetic mess which smoking makes has had surprisingly little effect on the habit. Perhaps it is because so many women smoke in this country that they are tolerant of the offensiveness of dirty ashtrays, impregnated curtains, and of fire risks. But harping on the extra cleanliness of a home where nobody smokes is the least attractive of arguments, conjuring visions of comfortless, sanitary, and unloving women – like Mrs Ogmore-Pritchard in *Under Milk Wood* who wants the sun to wipe his shoes before he comes into her immaculate, cheerless house. This is why the enthusiasts must go carefully. It is useless for a hostess to insist that her tasty cooking will be the better enjoyed by people with clean palates, true though this may be. Making one's guests feel uncomfortable or resented is no part of hospitality and I can see us going on emptying those ashtrays and cleaning up the dog-ends indefinitely. The most one can do is probably not to offer cigarettes, thereby at least suggesting one does not actually expect one's visitors to smoke.

But those of us for whom smoking brings no benediction are not likely to be the ablest propagandists. Above all, there must be no self-righteousness. For one of the elements in the build-up of smoking as a jolly, sociable, essential, and adult pastime has been the identification of many of its opponents with various forms of abstinence and unenvied asceticism, and not always with robust health. The citizen who wants to advise people not to smoke can so easily be disregarded along with the others who urge that one should not eat meat or drink alcohol or go to the pictures on

Sunday. Of course there is no reason why people with these strong beliefs should not seek to influence others. We are all trying to influence other people most of the time in the widest variety of ways, of which political propaganda is only one obvious example. But there is a difference, I think, between the sort of non-smoking campaign we need now and the existing moral prohibitions which some groups impose on this and other activities. The non-smoker, non-drinker Sabbatarian, for instance, has his own strong moral grounds for his decision and that is the main basis of his appeal to others. But no general approach to the public to cut down smoking on the basis that it is morally wrong is likely to have any appeal. Nor, in my view, should moralizing play a part. There is nothing to stop the individual who has a moral approach against smoking from propounding his theory – except the unlikelihood of success. Such an approach, however, would be intolerable from a government. Our rulers may forbid us crime, but they may not deny us our sins.

But the Government has the responsibility to regulate and reduce anti-social behaviour and to deal with nuisances to health. Nobody can keep a smelly drain on the grounds that it is his drain and he can do what he likes with his own. In a smokeless zone nobody may now have a smoky chimney. It is not too long a step from this to some restraint on the emission of smoke from one's person, especially in confined places which other people have to use.

What then can be done? A short-term scare programme may have a temporary effect but it will wear off if there is not a continuing and diverse effort to establish the idea that smoking is not essential, normal, pleasant, or helpful. Downright comprehensive prohibitions, as tried by Hitler in the name of health, have no history of success. (In pre-war Bremen, for example, smoking under the age of 18 was prohibited.) But there must be on the part of the Government and local authorities increasing restriction on the places where one can smoke. I would start with the Underground. This not only makes life more tolerable for non-smokers, but helps to break down the acceptance by the public of smoke as part of the environment.

This must be linked to a much more vigorous campaign about atmospheric pollution in all its forms. Meanwhile a great deal more work has to be done on finding out which people smoke and why. Clinics for addicts are being started and none of this work should be kept short of money or resources. And for an experimental period – say three years – I would like to see all advertising forbidden as in Italy. Instead we should use a similar amount of space and money to advertise the dangers of smoking. And just as the tobacco advertisers have used teen-age idols in many spheres and have romanticized the cigarette into all sorts of interesting circumstances, so I think society will need the help of well-known non-smokers. I do not mean this only in direct advertising. There is bound to be a cumulative effect if young people get used to seeing people they admire on television, in newspaper and magazine photographs without a cigarette.

I would forbid smoking on the stage as well as in the auditorium, unless smoking were an essential part of the plot or characterization. For instance, it would be ridiculous to attempt a dramatized presentation of Sherlock Holmes or Maigret without a pipe. But most of the time there is no dramatic reason for players to smoke on the stage – after all Hamlet has to manage for hours without a cigarette. I would apply this rule to television programmes. What is the use of propaganda about the virtue of not-smoking if clever father and mother figures on the 'Brains Trust', for instance, puff away all the time? The performers may feel helped by fiddling with cigarettes, or chewing their pipes. But they must do without, because this is just part of the build-up of the naturalness of smoking which has got to be broken down.

Some parents find it is best not to forbid smoking, because this only encourages smoking secretly or away from home. They hope that children will get over the novelty and that the less an issue is made the better. 'There's nothing in it,' is often the conclusion of the liveliest boys and girls.

Obviously school and home influences interact on each other, as well as all the public influences, which we have discussed earlier. But it is most important that discouragement to smoke should not be involved in young minds with other prejudices about abstentionist behaviour.

The Government could act also by stopping the issue of cheap cigarettes and tobacco to the forces. These have long been looked on as a 'perk', helping to make up for low pay. But would it not be a saving in the long run if the extra money were given? This could start by non-smokers being allowed to take the equivalent of the ration of 'smokes' in hard cash.

I do not think much is to be gained by further price increases. The confirmed smoker will merely cut down on other things, and the elderly will have to reduce what comfort they get from smoking. At the same time the well-paid young people will be least influenced – they are used to paying a lot for their pleasures and to make the cost of smoking prohibitive for them would need such a vast increase as to be socially unjust. Far better for them to conclude that, at present prices, smoking is a waste of money.

The restriction of smoking in public places, if only to the same extent as is accepted in other countries; a complete abstention from all forms of advertising for a trial period; a sustained campaign of public information; a deliberate attempt by parents, teachers, doctors, and others who have any influence to set some kind of tacit example; the abolition of cheap cigarettes for the forces – all these are needed, together with the general assault on air pollution.

I do not believe it is impossible to unhook the cigarette from the human face. This confidence must be the mainspring of all activity. Then gradually we may progress at least as far as Robert Burton (1577–1640) in *The Anatomy of Melancholy*:

Tobacco, divine, rare, superexcellent tobacco, which goes far beyond all their panaceas, potable gold and philosopher's stones, a sovereign remedy to all diseases – But, as it is commonly abused by most men, which take it as tinkers do ale, 'tis a plague, a mischief, a violent purger of goods, lands, health; hellish, devilish and damned tobacco, the ruin and overthrow of body and soul.

HOW TO STOP

Christopher Wood

THE history of the development of smoking as a socially
acceptable, even an esteemed habit, has been elaborated in
the preceding article. The question of changing the habit
involves both the individual smoker and society itself. The
interplay of these two is perhaps easier to appreciate if one
considers their relation to habits associated with taking
other drugs, the effects of which are more widely known.
In our society today excessive drinking, either in the form
of occasional drunkenness or of chronic alcoholism, is generally unacceptable. The weight of public opinion lends
its support in any attempt to help an individual stop excessive drinking. In the case of taking drugs like opium,
not only public opinion but also the law is on the side of
prevention. This differentiation between the acceptable,
the unacceptable, and the illegal is not universal in time or
place. There are today large majority communities, like
the Moslems, and small minority communities, like the
Mormons, to whom smoking is unacceptable. On the other
hand, there are groups among whom taking opium is both
normal and acceptable.

Is smoking a habit or an addiction? These two words are
apt to be used somewhat indiscriminately, but they are
both applicable. For the person who smokes only on certain occasions, either in company or after meals, and who
is not distressed if he is unable to do so, the word 'habit'
is appropriate. At the other end of the scale, the person
who would rather smoke than eat, who persists in smoking

even when he has a cold, and who craves cigarettes when
deprived, may fairly be described as an addict. There are,
of course, many stages between those with the casual habit
of smoking and a confirmed addict, just as there are many
stages between those who like an occasional glass of sherry
or beer and a chronic alcoholic. Those smoking ten cigarettes a day or less are seldom addicted, and those smoking
over thirty often are addicted, but the degree of addiction
does not appear to be directly related to the number
smoked. There are people who have smoked forty a day
for many years who are able to stop with remarkably little
difficulty or after-effect, much to their own surprise. There
are also those who smoke only ten or fifteen a day who find
stopping very distressing and who continue to crave for
them long afterwards. The difficulty experienced by others
in stopping smoking one or two cigarettes a day is not
evidence of pharmacological addiction but rather illustrates
how firmly a habit can become ingrained.

It is the habit of cigarette smoking with which we are
particularly concerned. In the first chapter it was shown
that smoking a pipe or cigar was relatively innocuous for
the smoker – though perhaps rather more offensive to
others. Comparatively few cigarette smokers are interested
in changing to a pipe or cigars except as a half-way stage
to stopping smoking altogether. The possibility of a differential tax that made pipe and cigar smoking relatively
cheaper is discussed later. The practical difficulties of
making cigarettes safer by means of filters or by removing
particular ingredients has been discussed in C. M. Fletcher's
article. It was shown that it will be twenty or more years
before any evidence is available showing whether these
measures will be effective. The present article is concerned
with the more immediate problem of how to stop cigarette
smoking altogether.

The changing of an established habit may be initiated either by a change in environment or by a personal decision. The city gentleman, accustomed to carrying his watch in his waistcoat pocket, may swelter for a while when he is in the tropics but will ultimately buy a wristwatch and make himself more comfortable by leaving his waistcoat at home. Alternatively, the man who has a comfortable trilby may decide to buy a bowler. This may be less comfortable to wear, and may to the unconverted look slightly ridiculous but with determination he will succeed in making the change.

In the same way, smoking habits may alter, either because the social environment exerts an influence or because an individual decides for himself. In either case, changing the habit is often not a simple or logical process. Merely accepting reasons why a habit should be changed does not imply willingness to do so, and it is here that the interplay between individual decision and social pressure is so important.

In our society today, smoking is more or less accepted at all ages from twelve upwards (and often tolerated below); and in most places, including in bed, on public transport, and in cinemas; and at all times, even while working or between the courses of a meal. Advertisers bombard us with their suggestions, and it is not regarded as unreasonable to spend £2 a week (£104 a year) on smoking. Therefore, the effort required by an individual to implement his decision to differ from the herd and not to smoke is considerable.

The propagandists of today are up against a 'chicken and egg' problem – until there are more non-smokers it is unlikely that our society will take any major steps towards reducing the acceptability of smoking, and, until it has done so, it will remain difficult for individuals to overcome a habit which remains socially acceptable.

This difficulty of changing habits is well known in the present-day field of preventive medicine. In the past there were diseases such as cholera, typhoid, and plague which could be dealt with by manipulating the environment – by providing better water supplies and drainage, and organizing refuse collection. This required relatively little understanding or cooperation from the population as a whole, which was therefore seldom obstructive. Other diseases such as smallpox, diphtheria, tetanus, measles, and more recently poliomyelitis, can be controlled if all, or at any rate most, members of the community will cooperate to the extent of exposing a small portion of their anatomy for vaccination on various occasions. However, diseases such as coronary artery disease, bronchitis, duodenal ulcer, lung cancer, and various forms of mental illness which are among the most common killing and disabling diseases today, can only be effected if members of the community are willing to change some of their ingrained eating, exercising, smoking, and working habits – indeed, to change in some important respects their way of life.

There is no simple way of overcoming this two-fold resistance to change in society and individuals over a short time, and, indeed it may be undesirable that changes of this nature should be undertaken too suddenly. Instead, we may perhaps gently tip the balance of what is acceptable to society a little against smoking and thereby encourage the efforts of those individuals who are genuinely trying to stop. As an increasing number of individuals manage to stop smoking, then the balance of what is and what is not acceptable may be pushed rather more firmly.

A slight change in the attitude of society has in fact taken place during the past few years, perhaps more noticeably since the publication of the Report on Smoking and Health by the Royal College of Physicians in March 1962. A few years ago, when discussing some of the health-hazards of smoking with those who were thinking of stopping, a standard reply was, 'If smoking is really as dangerous a habit as all that, why don't the Government do something about it?' – the implication being that as the Government had not actually done anything, what they were being told was probably untrue.

The Government has still not done anything very constructive, but, reluctantly and slowly, a succession of Ministers of Health are learning and becoming bolder. In 1954 the 'relationship' between smoking and cancer of the lung was accepted. In 1956 they spoke of the 'connexion' between the two. In 1957 they accepted the Medical Research Council's conclusion:

... That the most reasonable interpretation of the very great increase in deaths from lung cancer in males during the past twenty-five years is that a major part of it is caused by smoking tobacco, particularly heavy cigarette smoking.

But there has been no sense of urgency and the action taken has been negligible. After the Royal College of Physician's Report, the Minister of Health said in the House of Commons that the Government certainly accepted that the Report demonstrated authoritatively and crushingly the connexion between smoking and lung cancer and the more general hazards to health of smoking. Lord Hailsham said in the debate in the House of Lords:

We know, so far as any human being is concerned, that cigarette smoking, as it is now practised, is a cause of lung cancer in the countries and places where they are smoked. Whatever we do or do not do, we ought to act in this belief, and we cannot buy ourselves out of that fact by research; otherwise we deceive ourselves, and endanger others. We cannot afford to delude ourselves with alternative explanations which have been eliminated, nor with other hypotheses which, though possibly true, are not inconsistent with what I have said.

An unprecedented amount of publicity was given to the subject by the newspapers and television. Cigarette sales dropped by about twelve per cent. Tobacco shares fell.

In view of the size of the vested interest in the tobacco industry and the revenue derived from advertising in the press and on television, it is not surprising that the tobacco industry has fought back at these revelations, and that it has been abetted on occasions by some newspapers. A depressing example was set in this instance by *The Times*. In February 1956 a letter entitled 'Liability to Lung Cancer' asked the following question:

Many friends of mine who are now forty would stop smoking today if they were assured that by so doing their chances of contracting cancer of the lung were really reduced.... If someone qualified to reply to this question would do so it may possibly persuade thousands of men of forty to abandon the cigarette.

A reply to the Editor by Professor Bradford Hill and Dr Doll giving the information asked for, namely that the risk of developing lung cancer did diminish if people of forty stopped smoking, was not published by *The Times*. It appeared a little later – together with appropriate comment – in a leader on page 50 of *The British Medical Journal* for 3 March. One wonders whether the Editor of *The Times* would have found space for the reply had it indicated that continued smoking was harmless.

Following the publication of the Royal College of Physicians' Report *The Times* leader played it down and none of the letters sent to the Editor immediately afterwards was printed. One of their own correspondents submitted an account of the work of an anti-smoking clinic at the time. It was not included at the time.

This campaign of near silence by *The Times* has been complemented by the more sensational dailies who have produced a number of articles based on incorrect facts. When these errors have been pointed out their acknowedgement has been less than satisfactory.

A number of those who stopped smoking shortly after the Royal College of Physicians' Report and the publicity which followed soon started again, so that six months later the sale of cigarettes was down by only six per cent and the price of tobacco shares were back nearly to normal.

Even though the publicity given to the subject of smoking has not persuaded many to stop, a large number have been made aware that the dangers exist. This has gone a long way to removing the argument, 'As the Government has not done anything about smoking, it cannot be dangerous.'

The individual approach

What approach can be taken, therefore, with an individual who is considering whether to stop smoking? One point is clear. With current social acceptance of the habit, prohibition, such as during a period in hospital, which is enforced from without can have only a temporary effect. It is also a waste of time and effort to give any instruction on 'how' to stop smoking until the individual is convinced of the reason 'why' he intends to stop. The vague wish to stop is common to many smokers, but it falls a long way short of a real determination to do so. The conversion of this vague wish into determination is the most important first step. Once this is accomplished, the question of 'how' – by means of peppermints, elastic bands round

css-8

packets, dummy cigarettes, and the rest – becomes of secondary importance.

How, then, can the wish to stop smoking be consolidated? The relative significance of the several arguments will vary for different individuals. For instance, the person with a chronic cough who is just recovering from pneumonia is more likely to make the decision on health grounds, while the man who is wondering how he will manage to pay off his mortgage may be more influenced by economic considerations.

However, in all smokers there is a marked tendency to turn a blind eye to the direct personal implications and to rationalize smoking habits.

Health reasons for stopping smoking

It is often said, 'I know all about the risk to my health, but I think that the risk is worth it.' When this statement is true it should be accepted. Everyone has a right to choose what risks they take, however great they may be. However, often the statement really means, 'I have a nasty feeling that smoking is bad for my health, but I would rather not think about it.' With some of these people the bluff can be called and they can be asked to explain what they think the risk to their own health is. When this is done few get very far in personal terms. The bare fact that 23,000 people died of lung cancer last year in Great Britain often fails to impress an individual. When it is explained that this is the equivalent of one every twenty-five minutes or is four times as many as those killed on the roads, the significance is more apparent. The one-in-eight risk of dying of lung cancer for the man who smokes twenty-five or more cigarettes a day may be better appreciated if an analogy is used. If, when you boarded a plane, the girl at the top of the steps were to welcome you aboard with the greeting, 'I am pleased that you are coming with us – only one in eight of our planes crashes,' how many would think again, and make other arrangements? Alternatively, the analogy of Russian Roulette may appeal. The man smoking twenty-five or more a day runs the same risk between the ages of thirty and sixty as another who buys a revolver with 250 chambers and inserts one live bullet and on each of his birthdays spins the chamber, points the revolver at his head, and pulls the trigger. One of the difficulties in impressing these facts on people, is that, despite the current epidemic of lung cancer depicted in the first article, because it is a disease which kills relatively quickly, there are many who have as yet no experience of it among their family or friends.

This contrasts with the picture of chronic bronchitis, a knowledge of which is common to most people because it is a long-drawn-out disease and death usually only follows many years of suffering. However, most smokers reserve the term chronic bronchitis for elderly people with severe breathlessness. They fail to appreciate that this is only the last stage of a disease which probably began twenty years ago with a chronic productive morning cough which they may themselves have, but which they prefer to call by the euphemism of 'smoker's cough'.

The readiness with which people will suggest an association between disease and air pollution by chimney smoke or by diesel fumes provides an interesting contrast to their reluctance to accept the relation to cigarette smoking. One of the important differences between the two being that 'they' ought to do something about air pollution, while 'I' would have to change smoking habits. That those living in cities have a greater liability to lung cancer and bronchitis is true, but the difference between town and country is considerably less than the difference between smoking and not smoking. It is also likely that town smoke and cigarette

smoke are cumulative in their effects. It therefore follows
that if one is exposed to the danger of living in a town it
is all the more important to refrain from augmenting the
risk by smoking. While there is no doubt that the black,
stinking fumes from a poorly maintained diesel lorry are
most unpleasant, there is as yet no evidence of any direct
harm. Mechanics in garages and London traffic policemen,
who might be expected to show an effect if there is one, do
not appear to have any excess of lung cancer.

Describing the part played by smoking in these diseases, or
in any other such as coronary artery disease, tuberculosis,
rupture, or duodenal ulcer, in personal terms which could be
appreciated by and would be particularly relevant to the individual concerned, would not be justifiable unless a remedy
was available. There is, in fact, ample evidence to refute the
commonly held view, 'Well – it is too late for me to do anything about it.' The facts show that the risk of developing
lung cancer decreases strikingly in those who stop smoking
in comparison with those who continue. The improvement
in symptoms in bronchitis is often striking, and in some
early cases it is probable that permanent cure follows.

Economic reasons for stopping smoking

The economic aspect of smoking can be interpreted in
many different ways, but the reluctance to consider it in
personal terms closely resembles the reluctance to consider
health risks in personal terms. At one end of the scale, the
fact that the Government revenue from tax on tobacco is
of the order of £900 million is incomprehensible to most.
Such numbers are used by astronomers and those who make
machines to reach the moon. The effect of their mention
to an ordinary mortal is to make him feel that by smoking
he is paying his share! At the other end of the scale, there
are few who can multiply 1s. 11d. or 4s. 6d. by 2 or 7 or

365. Self-delusion takes on an almost wilful aspect. For instance, many who buy a packet of twenty cigarettes every
day will swear that they only smoke fifteen because they
always have five left the next morning! For many, there is
a ritual of buying cigarettes in small quantities frequently.
This helps the delusion of total cost.

To get some understanding of the personal financial aspects it is necessary to add up what is spent in the morning,
the afternoon, the day, the week, the month, the year, and
during a lifetime. 1s. 11d. in the morning and again in the
afternoon is 3s. 10d. Five days a week this is 19s. 2d.
Thirty cigarettes for Saturdays and Sundays is 11s. 6d.
making approximately 30s. a week or £6 a month. Then
there are parties and holidays and Christmas to be thrown
in, making £80 per year. This rate of smoking is often
reached at around seventeen years of age, so that by thirty
£1,000 has been spent and by the age of retirement the
figure is approaching £4,000 at current prices.

According to age and inclination these sums must be
contrasted with other items of expenditure such as records,
radios, bicycles, cameras, holidays, sports cars, and houses.
These popular items should be compared with the fact that
at current prices, a cancer of the lung usually costs around
£2,500, though cheaper specimens are not unknown! It is
this that has given rise to the cynical name for a packet
of cigarettes in vogue among some medical students – 'a
3s. 10d. do-it-yourself cancer kit'!

Other reasons for stopping smoking

There are others who are prepared to accept the cost and
health-risks involved, but who for various reasons do not like
to feel that they cannot stop smoking. These reasons may be
associated with guilt feelings about addiction or a lack of
self-control. These personal reasons of a moral nature are

the happy hunting-ground of the crusader who is often more concerned with his crusade than with smoking. On the other hand, some people are concerned with the example they set to others, particularly their children. Help can be given to these people by confirming the impression – for which there is considerable evidence – that parental influence is of major importance in the development of smoking habits in children.

Having passed from the stage of wishing to stop smoking to the stage of being determined to do so, there are many who have then gone on to do it by themselves. Many doctors, who as a group cannot often be held up as an example, have done this. Two-thirds of them used to smoke cigarettes and now only approximately one-third do. It may be presumed that they have done this because they are in a better position to know the medical facts and to see ill-effects at first-hand. It may also be presumed that many of them wish to set an example to others – though this is unfortunately not true of them all.

How can help be given to those who are wavering on the brink of decision? So far little has been done and there is an urgent need for investigation and experiment.

In an attempt to provide help, pamphlets and books have been written, gramophone records have been made, medical and psychological consultations have been held, and various anti-smoking clinics have been set up. The British Anti-Smoking Society – a group originally concerned with the rights of non-smokers – started discussion groups. A 'Smokers Anonymous' was formed and clinics have been run for those referred to them for medical reasons.

Anti-smoking clinics

Some anti-smoking clinics consist of a group of ten or fifteen people wishing to stop smoking who meet together once a week under the guidance of a doctor. The first stage of the method used to help them consists of an explanation and a discussion in the kind of personal terms already described of all the reasons why those present may wish to stop smoking. This is then followed by getting each person to describe in some detail their own smoking history, including why and when they started, how the habit grew, the times of day and special occasions at which they most wish to smoke, and the reasons for which they do it. An attempt is made by gentle prompting to bring out as many different patterns of smoking and reasons for it as possible. That there are differences comes as a surprise to many. Some differences of technique, such as which end of. a cigarette is put in the mouth after tapping, are unimportant. Others, such as the difference between the person who keeps a cigarette in his mouth all the time with one eye half-closed and who often does not inhale, and the person who keeps his cigarette on the edge of the bench or in the ashtray, only picking it up two or three times for a long draw, may give clues as to how they should attempt to stop. Another important difference which is often marked is the time at which a cigarette is wanted most. There are those who say that they cannot concentrate or get on with their work without one – the writer who cannot write unless he smokes, the bricklayer or the machine operator who lights up when there is a tricky job to do, and the salesman who produces cigarettes at the critical stage of negotiation. On the other hand there are those who say that they cannot relax without a smoke – after meals or at home in the evening – or who smoke when there is nothing else to do, or when they are bored.

As a result of hearing other people's reasons for smoking, many begin to question some of their own and begin to wonder whether they have not been rationalizing.

In particular they may begin to question whether a cigarette really does 'soothe the nerves'. There are many occasions in the day when people are anxious or puzzled, upset or worried. Do those who take a cigarette become soothed more quickly or not? The idea that a cigarette is 'sociable', 'helps break the ice', 'makes a party go' may also be challenged, and some of the anti-social aspects, such as the dirt and litter, the stained fingers and smelly breath, may be put forward. Many will state that the taste is pleasurable, but on careful questioning few will maintain that many cigarettes are smoked for the taste. The greater the total number smoked, the fewer are enjoyed for themselves rather than as part of the pleasure of fulfilling a habit.

Having first helped people towards understanding why they should stop smoking and then undermined their ideas on why they are actually doing so – the next stage is to show them that it is possible to stop. This is easy in a group clinic which meets weekly, as there are people at different stages. An element of competition often occurs: 'If she can, why shouldn't I?' – 'I would never have thought that he had the will-power!' Having demonstrated that stopping is possible, those who have managed it describe how they have done it, what they feel like, and what they intend to do next. Some will have horrific stories of their struggle, others will say that they are amazed that they have succeeded with no real anguish at all. If anyone with chest symptoms has stopped, the almost immediate improvement in their cough will be added to the other list of benefits, real or imaginary, that are commonly described: food beginning to taste better, breathing becoming easier, a sense of smell returning, and a general feeling of better health. These accounts will reinforce the intentions of others to try to stop.

It is important to harness the self-righteousness of recent converts to helping those who are about to stop by encouraging them to continue attendance at the clinic. This is better than letting them exasperate their friends. Also there is a dangerous period after three to six weeks when someone may become over-confident of success and be tempted to have 'just one' – this may easily result in a rapid return to former smoking habits. If such a person is continuing to attend the clinic the thought of 'letting the group down' may be sufficient to enable him to resist the desire to smoke even this single one.

The question of whether to cut down smoking or to stop altogether is complex. As far as is known there is no 'threshold' below which smoking is safe. The health-risk and the financial cost both get progressively less in relation to the number of cigarettes smoked. If a person has never smoked more than two or three cigarettes a day, there is little to worry about. If, however, a regular smoker of twenty, thirty, or forty a day cuts down his smoking, the chances of his going back to heavy smoking are far greater than if he stops altogether. No one who has just cut down his smoking will believe that he will go back, but, when some worry or accident or party comes along, the person who has failed to make the complete break is much more likely to increase his smoking again than the person who has changed to being a non-smoker is likely to start again. Though two or three cigarettes may be really enjoyed by the person who has never smoked more, they are no more than tantalizing to the ex-smoker of thirty or forty a day. Whether somebody decides to make a complete break all at once, or prefers to halve his consumption each week, is a matter of individual preference. However, attempts to stop which are spread out over more than a few weeks are seldom successful.

The tricks of stopping

So far, in the description of a group clinic, no mention has been made of 'how' to stop smoking. The omission is deliberate. A number of people, including even those who decide to attend a clinic, want to be 'given the treatment', to 'collect the pill', to 'have the injection', or to 'be hypnotized'. They want somebody else to stop smoking for them. None of these methods succeeds in the absence of the earlier stages of the process described. People may attend a clinic for several weeks before the wish to stop is converted into determination. When this happens and is accompanied by an appreciation that it can be done, the battle is more than half-won and some of the adjuncts to completing the process may be discussed. Because of the different ways of smoking and the different reasons for doing so, what helps one person may be of no use to another. Surprisingly frequently, however, someone will say, 'The only thing that helped me was what so-and-so suggested', even though it may sound ridiculous to others. For many a definite plan of campaign should be thought out.

It is important to choose the right time to stop smoking. It is a mistake to try at a time of particular stress or just before Christmas, but the date for stopping should not be put off for too long. If the greatest urge to smoke is at work, the beginning of the week-end is a good time to stop – if at home, then start on a Monday. Before the date of starting it may help to change the brand of cigarette and to stop smoking for one or two hours during each day, say before ten in the morning. More should not be taken on than can be achieved with certainty. Therefore, rather than approaching a change of habit with a 'sign the pledge' attitude, a decision not to smoke for one day is often better. This can be done by anyone. At the end of the day a decision not to smoke the next day may be taken and so on until a week is up. This may then be doubled and doubled again.

Part of the planning should include deciding what will be done instead of smoking. Starting with the first smoke at the beginning of the day, think out alternative activities. For someone who lights a cigarette first thing on waking, it may help to pour a small glass of bitter lemon the night before. On drinking this, the dry astringent taste relieves the urge to smoke for a little while. Someone who smokes on a bus to work should ride downstairs for a while. If a cigarette is enjoyed at a tea break or after a meal, seek out someone who does not smoke and join him for a few days. The person who likes a cigarette in his mouth for most of the time is more likely to be helped by sucking something else – boiled sweets, fruit gums, or peppermints. On the other hand those who take long draws on a cigarette may find the urge discouraged by biting on a clove, which will leave a hot taste, incompatible with smoking, for a few minutes. For those whose greatest urge to smoke is when they wish to sit down and relax at home in the evening, the task is more difficult. There is nothing for it but a conscious effort to do some of those things that have been put off time and time again – doing these extra things for a few days may help to pass the crucial period. A strong urge to have a cigarette with a drink means either avoiding the drink or having it in a place and in company where the temptation can be resisted.

At the end of a week it is important that some tangible reward for the week's work should be obtained. Some extravagance should be bought with the money saved.

Medical aids to stopping

What help can be given by drugs or hypnosis to those endeavouring to stop smoking? Of two things there can be no doubt. There is no drug which can safely be adminis-

tered to a smoker which will make him stop if he does not
wish to do so. However, stopping smoking is no different
from many other situations. Belief in the effectiveness of a
certain preparation or in what is prescribed by someone will
undoubtedly give it some value. There is a large gap of uncertainty between these two generally accepted statements.
A drug which has often been tried is a preparation of lobeline, which is chemically very similar to nicotine and is
given as a substitute. There have been conflicting reports
about its efficacy. When lobeline tablets have been tested by
the 'double-blind' method – in which they have been compared with dummy tablets by an observer who did not know
which person was taking which – no beneficial effect was
found on one occasion, and some benefit on another. On
the other hand, injections of lobeline are thought to be
effective by a group of Swedish doctors who have used
it with at least short-term success on many thousands
of patients attending their clinics over the past few
years.

Other non-specific drugs have also been used for their
general effect, such as for sedation or stimulation, or even
both at the same time. Any benefit that these may have is
only marginal.

Hypnosis has been tried and been found to be successful
by some. It must be remembered, however, that many succeed in stopping smoking without hypnosis, and how important a boost this gives is very difficult to ascertain. Few
who have been hypnotized smoke again within twenty-four
hours. This is not a long time, but the first day or two are
the most difficult and any help through this period is not to
be despised. It is, however, quite impracticable to consider
hypnosis on a very large scale.

The success of the methods used for helping individuals
or small groups to stop smoking has varied. Measured

ver a short time, the clinics in Sweden run by Dr Ejrup claim a 98 per-cent success 76 per-cent stopped, and 2 per-cent cut down to less than twenty-five per cent of what was smoked before. Others have claimed a sixty-per-cent and others no more than a thirty-per-cent success. The success-rate depends to a large extent on the reasons which first brought the smoker to the clinic. If the smoker wants' to stop and has elected to go on his own, the success-rate tends to be much higher than if he has been referred by his doctor because he 'should' stop. With the exception of the Swedish clinics the numbers attending have so far been small. It is clear, therefore, that much remains to be done to improve the techniques of helping individuals and in making such help more widely available. But however valuable this may be for the individual, clinics of this nature will never have more than a marginal effect on the smoking habits of the community as a whole, except in so far as their existence influences public opinion and those who frame our laws.

The future

When the balance of public opinion does come down a little more firmly in favour of limiting the habit of cigarette smoking, what can be done?

I would like to see frequent and regular announcements of the death-toll associated with cigarette smoking so that the danger is kept constantly in the public eye. The comparative energy behind the road-safety campaign makes an interesting comparison with the absence of any official national anti-smoking programme. Road deaths per mile travelled have fallen sharply since the war, while total annual deaths have only risen from 4,000 to 6,000 (the rise of recorded lung-cancer deaths in the similar period has been from 3,000 to 23,000). Before each Bank Holiday period the Minister of Transport or another public figure appeals for careful driving. During the holiday frequent bulletins of the latest death-tolls are given with comparative figures for previous years. And yet during each of these holidays more people die as a result of cigarette-smoking than from road accidents. On an average, the annual toll of cigarette deaths increases by 1,000 each year. It is a peculiar and sad fact that so far in their respect the Ministry of Health have fallen far short of the Ministry of Transport in their concern for public safety.

There should also, I believe, be an extension of the times and places in which smoking is not allowed. This extension should be based on hygiene and fire considerations as well as on its nuisance-value to others. It might include in the first instance food shops, cinemas, and public transport.

Cigarette advertising could be prohibited or required to observe a more honest standard. The prohibition of the advertising of a product, the sale of which is not illegal, is perhaps illogical, although this has been done in Italy. I would prefer to see regulations that required the proportions of the various ingredients of tobacco products to be stated on the containers (as they are with some medicines), with a warning of the possible effects of overdosage. If this were done, much advertising would cease without its being prohibited. However, in Czechoslovakia, where there is no advertising, the increase in tobacco consumption has continued in the last ten years at a rate very similar to that in Great Britain, where many millions are spent each year on advertising. If cigarette advertising in this country *is* effective in increasing total consumption it would be better for it to be curtailed in the interests of public health. An attempt should also be made to limit the almost unconscious popularizing and glamourizing of cigarette smoking by public figures and by stage and television personalities.

In the long run, I believe the most effective method of reducing smoking will be to treat it as a luxury rather than a common necessity. It should be removed from the list of items on which the cost of living index is based and a much higher tax gradually applied. Gin drinking was a serious menace while it was cheap. Tax was levied so that gin drinking ceased to be something done by many people much of the time and became a luxury indulged in occasionally. Hip flasks went out. An announcement that the tax on twenty cigarettes would be increased by a shilling a year until they cost £1 a packet would help many to reduce their smoking to one after meals and a few at a party. At the same time the mechanism of taxation might be changed. We do not tax barley, hops, or grapes, but the alcoholic content of the end product. In the same way, instead of an excise tax on the import of tobacco, a retail tax based on the form of the end product – cigarettes, cigars, and pipe tobacco – graduated according to the health risk associated with it – could be instituted. It has been suggested that the tax might also be related to the nicotine content. Nicotine is not the only or necessarily the most harmful ingredient of cigarettes and it is not closely related to taste. It is however the constituent that causes addiction. If cheaper cigarettes with the same taste but a lower nicotine content were made available, some people would buy them. After a while it might be hoped that some of those smoking cigarettes with reduced habit-forming constituents would find it easier to stop altogether or to smoke in moderation. If however cost is the limiting factor in the number smoked, there is the possibility that because cigarettes with a low nicotine content were cheaper, more would be smoked and a greater dose of the tars thought to be dangerous would be taken out.

The difficulty of stopping the habit of smoking once it is

acquired emphasizes the extreme importance of preventing young people from starting. Here again, one is up against a 'chicken-and-egg' problem because example is more effective than exhortation. However, laws concerning the sale of tobacco to juveniles should be enforced and re-enforced by the prohibition of slot machines selling cigarettes. Later, perhaps, the possession of cigarettes in a public place could be made an offence for those under age, as it is in Jersey.

Approximately a quarter of a million people have so far died in this country as a result of smoking cigarettes. It would appear that the very scale of the slaughter has numbed public response. One hesitates to guess how many more will die before the urgency of the situation is appreciated and more than half-hearted measures are instituted to curb this menace.